Lean Empowerment and Respect for People

There are two pillars of a Lean Management System: Continuous Improvement and Respect for People. Most books about Lean Production have focused overwhelmingly on Continuous Improvement and fail to treat Respect for People as an equal pillar. It is overlooked or understated, resulting not in a Lean house, but in a lean-to structure. It is our responsibility to level out the structure once again.

The study of people is messy and exciting. It demands that we explore multiple interdisciplinary studies, including psychology, sociology, philosophy, and even theology. This book runs a parallel course with Lean Production but has a different goal. Instead of production, efficiency, and financial gains, our goal is to understand the reasons why staff come to work in the morning. We can only understand a system when we understand its people. They own the culture.

Lean must therefore evolve from a Production System in to an Empowerment System.

Lean Production will no longer serve the contemporary workforce; knowledge workers, if you are reading this, you are likely a knowledge worker who deserves more than a repackaging of the same ideas. You are not a line worker, and your system should not treat you as such. Therefore, we need a new system. One that prioritizes Respect for People over Continuous Improvement. Leaders in this system must recognize belonging and psychological safety as preconditions to process innovation. New definitions of value and waste—the staples of Lean philosophy—must take on a more human face and propel the change of culture. We must flip Lean on its head for the sake of our modern workforce.

Lean Empowerment and Respect for People

The Evolution of Lean Production Systems

Trevor Gundlach

Routledge
Taylor & Francis Group

A PRODUCTIVITY PRESS BOOK

First published 2024
by Routledge
605 Third Avenue, New York, NY 10158

and by Routledge
4 Park Square, Milton Park, Abingdon, Oxon, OX14 4RN

Routledge is an imprint of the Taylor & Francis Group, an informa business

ISBN: 978-1-032-64412-7 (hbk)
ISBN: 978-1-032-64411-0 (pbk)
ISBN: 978-1-032-64413-4 (ebk)

DOI: 10.4324/9781032644134

Typeset in Garamond
by SPi Technologies India Pvt Ltd (Straive)

For Kayla
Whose love and support give me the freedom to explore my crazy ideas.

For Mom & Dad
Who, through my upbringing, inspired my interest in organization and stable processes.
You have taught me, through your actions, what it means to be a servant leader.

Contents

Figures

Acknowledgments

The content for this book was inspired by countless meetings and conversations that I shared with co-workers at Kettering Health Medical Group. I thank all of you who gave me grace and pushed me. I am especially grateful for the leaders who trusted me to build an innovative system to give our staff a voice. And none of this would have been possible without the trust and daily challenges from our Peer Experts and frontline staff. Please continue to hold me accountable!

Thank you, Patrick McKeone and Lukonde Mwinga, my first team, and unofficial co-creators of the Lean Empowerment System. Your leadership influence is wider than you'll ever realize. Thank you for picking up the phone anytime I call with random ideas and for supporting me as a young leader.

A special shout-out to my mentors, Mike Snow and Joe Nicosia. I appreciate your reminders to connect meaning and purpose to the important work of leadership.

Thank you to Dr. Ray Poelstra, whose philosophical conversations over BLTs and French onion soup fill my heart with laughter and inspiration.

Thank you to my editorial team at Productivity Press for your partnership and guidance.

Most importantly, I thank my wife, Kayla, who has supported me through the research, writing, and editing of this book. Thank you for giving me the first and last hour of each day to hide away in my office with a nose buried in a book or eyes glued to a screen. You are a wonderful mother, talented nurse, and a beautiful friend.

About the Author

Trevor Gundlach is an author, philosopher, and healthcare leader. He holds an M.A. in Theological Studies from the University of Dayton and an M.B.A. in Project Management from Indiana Wesleyan University. Trevor is the author of *Barstool Theology: Crafting the Good Life* and founder of the Lean Empowerment System. He leads a team of project managers, process coaches, and clinical educators at Kettering Health Medical Group in Southwest Ohio.

Empowerment gets Trevor out of bed in the morning, and a cup of pour-over coffee takes it from there. He lives in a delicate balance between rigorous philosophy and approachable storytelling. Trevor's vocation is to help others find meaning and purpose in the workplace through systems and processes. He draws energy and inspiration from years of work as a teacher, campus minister, and director of spiritual retreats. Now, he channels that same energy into the boardroom, guiding teams of executive leaders with clarity and direction, or in the coffee shop, mentoring the leaders of the next generation. Trevor is passionate about connecting work to strategy and creating sustainable systems to support the change that our frontline staff demand.

Trevor lives in Dayton, Ohio with his wife, Kayla, and their three children, Willow, Noah, and Porter. They find joy in home renovation, time in nature, and cooking.

Introduction

Many Lean books expand the reader's understanding of the Production System first popularized by Toyota. You may already be familiar with the common ideas of Lean, Six Sigma, and Kaizen, to name a few. These labels represent a system of production whose aim is to increase the bottom line by means of efficiency. Staff must reduce non-value-added work (waste) and increase value-added work.

There are two traditional pillars of a Lean Management System: **Continuous Improvement** and **Respect for People** (Figure 0.1). Most books about Lean Production have focused overwhelmingly on Continuous Improvement and fail to treat Respect for People as an equal and interdependent pillar. It is overlooked or understated, resulting in not a Lean system, but a lean-to. It is our responsibility to level out the structure once again.

But the study of people is messy and exciting. It demands that we explore multiple interdisciplinary studies, including psychology, sociology, philosophy, and even theology. This book runs a parallel course with Lean Production but has a different goal. Instead of production, efficiency, and financial gains, our goal is to understand the reasons why staff come to work in the morning. We can only understand a system when we understand its people. They own the culture.

Alfie Kohn, renowned psychologist, and motivation theorist, argues that "at some point we may have to decide what matters most."[1] So we start this book with a decision: Do we focus on Production or something else?

This leads us to define our thesis:

DOI: 10.4324/9781032644134-1

Figure 0.1 Two pillars of lean management.

Lean must evolve from a production system to an empowerment system

Setting Empowerment as the goal – instead of Production – opens the door for a fresh perspective on decades-old ideas, all of which formed during specific contexts. For example, Training Within Industry (TWI) was created during World War II in the United States to create standards and train thousands of civilians to work in factories as the current workforce left for battle. The Toyota Production System (TPS) and its many adjunct philosophies (Poka-Yoke, Kaizen, Kata, etc.) spread in response to scarcity in post-World War II Japan. Standardization fueled the Industrial Revolution.[2] Six Sigma was founded on Walter Shewhart's science of statistical control and allowed efficient time studies (Taylorism) for the 20th-century industrial boom.

But these diverse faces of Lean Production will no longer serve the contemporary workforce: Knowledge workers. If you are reading this, you are likely a knowledge worker who deserves more than a repackaging of the same ideas. You are not a line worker, and your system should not treat you as such. Therefore, we need a new system. One that prioritizes Respect for People *over* Continuous Improvement. Leaders in this system must recognize belonging and psychological safety as preconditions to process innovation.[3] New definitions of value and waste, the staples of Lean philosophy, must take on a more human face and propel the change of culture. We must flip Lean on its head for the sake of our modern workforce.

Outline

This book is divided into two parts: The **Theory** of the Lean Empowerment System and the **Practice** of the Lean Empowerment System. Part I will equip readers with an interpretive lens through which the application of the Lean Empowerment System makes sense. We will see how the threads of a Lean Empowerment System are more deeply woven through the founders of Lean Management than many contemporary publications.

We begin Chapter 1 with the definitions of virtue and vice and how the theories of each can help us understand the work of improvement. We contrast the Vices of Production (Heroes, Management, Projects, and Urgency) with the corresponding Virtues of Empowerment (Ordinary People, Peer Problem Solving, Kaizen, and Design). Lean Systems that depend on Vices of Production are self-limiting and can only be liberated if they shift energy toward the four virtues.

Chapter 2 is a reflection on common failures that organizations might experience when launching a Lean Production System. These include Improvement Projects, Quality Control (QC) Circles, and Daily Management (Kamishibai). The stories in each section are either firsthand accounts (fictionalized for anonymity) or secondhand stories from Lean literature. Each shortcoming has a corresponding lesson learned that provides a contextual framework for the Lean Empowerment System in Part II.

Part II is the tangible application of the ideas presented in Part I. We start by defining the new model of improvement as **"An organic system of Lateral Leaders who improve Standard Work with a Kaizen Suggestion System."** The four following chapters break apart this definition into system, people, process, and technology.

Chapter 4 (System) explores the idea of a self-organizing and **organic system**. First, the theories of Reductionism and Systems Thinking are presented as complementary lenses for readers to better understand system models. We explore the three components of a system: elements, relationships between elements, and the purpose of a system. With this shared language, we then present three common systems models: Open-Source Systems, Microsystems, and Complex Adaptive Systems (CAS). The mechanistic language of Production is replaced with the more appropriate organic language of Empowerment.

Chapter 5 (People) introduces the novel role of **Lateral Leaders** in the Empowerment System and the weekly cadence of the Process Improvement Team. The Lateral Leader is the most important addition to Lean thinking and is the reason why the Empowerment System thrives. Here we will introduce eight titles by which the Lateral Leader has been known in various primary and secondary Lean sources throughout the past century.

Chapter 6 (Process) familiarizes readers with methods to **improve Standard Work with a Kaizen Suggestion System**. Readers must first understand the difference between Kaizen and Innovation as culturally distinct packages for improvement. This is followed by a history lesson of the Suggestion System through Training Within Industry (TWI) and Psychological Safety. All of this sets a foundation for an exposition on standard work and the critical role it plays in the Lean Empowerment System. We first must follow the SDCA (Standardize, Do, Check, Act) process to write Standard Work, then the PDCA (Plan, Do, Check, Act) process to improve Standard Work, and conclude with a novel review of standard work for leaders.

Finally, Chapter 7 (Technology) assesses the role of physical and digital technology in the Lean Empowerment System. This includes tools for accountability, including data and strategy, and tools for personal development, including mentorship and digital collaboration platforms.

Allow me to introduce a tool that you can use to understand Lean Empowerment for the first time. It is called the Wesleyan Quadrilateral, a tool used by theologians when they scrutinize new ideas in academia. The Quadrilateral has four sides: Scripture (Literature), History, Philosophy, and Experience. We must first analyze a new idea through the **literary** sources on the topic, both primary and secondary. Then, the idea must be positioned in the **historical** narrative to ensure the evolution over time is warranted. Third, the merit of the idea must follow reason and carry **philosophical** legitimacy. And finally, the idea must have a human face and capture the real **experience** of people doing the work. Let us slightly adapt the same quadrilateral to place our content in context. Only then can we give this book a home in the rich narrative of Lean thought.

Literary Context: Primary and Secondary Sources

The current landscape of Lean literature is at the same time both expansive and limited. Primary sources are limited to a few key names: Deming, Juran, Ohno, Shingo, Ishikawa, and Imai. Their respective books spanned from the mid-1900s to late 1900s and were packaged not as "Lean" but firsthand recollections of improvement and production methodologies. These ideas carried into the early 2000s, when "Lean" was first defined as a concept and its tools entered the spotlight. The genre had a breakthrough with Liker's book *The Toyota Way* and Womack, Jones, and Roos book *The Machine that Changed the World*. But the focus quickly shifted from the work of primary sources to certain ideas or themes that captured the imagination of leaders who were looking for quick wins. The Lean books of the early 2010s, celebrated by the Shingo Prize, tell the stories of various companies who successfully applied the theories of Lean that were taught in the preceding decades. And, most recently, the books of the 2015-2020 period are either encyclopedic repackaging of Lean terms, or a further narrowing of specific Lean tools (Process Mapping, Kata, Kanban, etc.) and their application to specific fields (IT, Healthcare, Human Resources, etc.).

We must uncover the original intent of what is now defined as "Lean." Only then can we creatively build on the philosophy of the founders instead of repackaging the same old Lean tools. Depending on how you look at it, this is both an introduction and advanced course in Lean. But it may look nothing like what you have commonly known as Lean. Our "uniquely branded Lean business system," like the Lean giants of Danaher, Toyota, Honeywell, and Pentair, is simply the result of applied theories.[4] And, like Toyota, we will draw upon the original voices who consulted their process (Deming, Juran, Ishikawa) instead of using Toyota as the primary source. We must "learn from" Toyota instead of "be[ing] like" Toyota. Keep in mind that Toyota is a secondary source, not a primary source as we are made to believe.[5]

Historical Context: Mass, Craft, and Lean Production Systems

Many people believe the word "lean" was an intentionally chosen term to symbolize a minimalist system devoid of waste or fat. But the etymology of "lean" is far less exciting: it is simply an antonym to the word "mass." This seemingly obvious but overlooked fact can help us understand the context for a Lean Empowerment System that is further contrasted with a Mass Production System or Craft Production System.

An organization becomes truly Lean when it is freed from the grasps of Mass and Craft Production. It must shed elements of Mass and Craft production that bled into the model over time as unchallenged artifacts. They have no place in an Empowerment System that caters to knowledge workers. Therefore, we must understand both Mass and Craft Production to better identify these elements and place Lean in its historical context.

Aristotle is attributed to a popular theory of virtue that places two vices – deficiency and excess – on two ends of a line-segment. He then placed

Virtue as the golden mean, or middle point, between these two vices (We will explore this further in Chapter 1). For the sake of this book, we must understand Lean as the golden mean between Mass Production (excess) and Craft Production (deficiency). Let us better understand some basic elements of each Production System before introducing a Lean Empowerment System.

	Craft Production	Mass Production	Lean Production
Staff	Highly Skilled Irreplaceable	Unskilled Disposable	Cross-Functional Teams
Product Flow	Single Item	Batch and Queue	Parallel Processes and Pull Systems (Kanban)
Productivity	Low	High	High
Cost	High	Medium	Low
Quality	High	Low	High

Mass Production System

The assembly lines of the early 20th century automotive industry are symbolic of mass production. Henry Ford popularized the mechanical assembly line to move items from station to station, allowing workers to focus on a single job instead of many. The Industrial Revolution was fueled by this new method of production that exists in our modern age.

I vaguely (and not too fondly) recall my first job in high school working at a factory for a major supplier of household cleaners. This opportunity was described to me as a privilege since my father worked as a Product Developer for the company. I remember unloading boxes of triggers for window cleaner into one chute and then monitoring their installation onto bottles as they sped through an automated system. My job was to unclog any major jams or remove products that failed to meet quality standards. I worked for six weeks before heading off to college, never to return. Upon further reflection, I realized I was unskilled, disposable, and cheap, but I could unclog the bottle machine and move products along the assembly line. A mass production system doesn't sugarcoat its needs or act like anything it isn't. It is purely mechanical and borrows language from engineering. People and technology are equally cogs in the machine, and the goal is output.

Craft Production System

My wife's late grandpa owned a medical practice in a small town (Population: 1200) in rural Ohio. I remember seeing his traveling medicine bag – a leather case with a single deep pocket – on display at his funeral. It was an artifact of healthcare in a different era. My father-in-law, who inherited his medical practice, explained how his father could carry anything he needed in this bag as he visited the homes of his patients. He was not tethered to an EMR (Electronic Medical Record), a team of medical staff to assist with chart prep, a call center to manage referrals, or digital knowledge bases of best practices. Instead, he was highly skilled and difficult to replace, a master of his craft and a god-like figure who dealt in the business of life and death. Everything he knew was owed to his education, residency, and knowledge passed down from others in the craft. He was an artist, only to be replaced by another artist.

A Craft Production System functions at the expense of time, cost, and sustainability. The product is unique to the builder. It is a work of art. For this reason, it is hard, and sometimes impossible, to replicate. This and many other high standards are held by customers of Craft Production. They are willing to wait longer and spend more on something that is unique. Or they justify the initial investment in a higher quality item assuming it will need to be replaced less frequently. Craft Production is the antithesis of Mass Production.

Lean Production System

Recall from the Introduction how the success of Lean production is built on two pillars: Continuous Improvement and Respect for People.[6] The goal is to reduce waste (non-value-added activities) and increase value-added activities. Value is defined by the customer and must meet three conditions: it changes the function or form of the activity, it must be done right the first time, and the customer must be willing to pay for the change. A Lean Production System focuses more on processes than results, since practitioners know that a better process will result in better outcomes. Process improvement is a means to the end of better outcomes.

The second pillar of Lean production is Respect for People. The people of an organization must be viewed as an investment, not a liability. Sustainable improvement is only possible if staff are engaged in efforts to reduce waste and increase value-added activities. Each person is invited to join multidisciplinary teams that are equipped with Standard Work and Data to identify problems and drive change. They are valued like artists in Craft Production but follow Standards like frontline staff in Mass Production. And, like the pillar of Continuous Improvement, Respect for People is a means to the end of better outcomes.

Lean Empowerment System

I used to work as a campus minister at the University of Dayton. My apartment was in the basement of a freshman co-ed residence hall in the middle of campus, and I was bound to run into students anytime I walked out the door. Since it was a Catholic university, and due to my title as a campus minister, I was frequently approached by students with questions pertaining to faith or theology. The questions differed depending on the season of the school year – orientation, midterms, breaks, finals, etc. – and I was constantly seeking new ways to encourage students to think creatively about the everchanging seasons of their lives.

The season of Lent (the forty days leading up to Easter) is known as a time of prayer, fasting, and almsgiving to reflect on the death and resurrection of Jesus. During this time, students often ask each other the question "What are you giving up for Lent?" The usual responses include chocolate, coffee, hot showers, and procrastinating, to name a few. But I knew this was only half of the purpose for Lent; we do not fast for the sake of fasting alone. **We fast so we can feast**. We experience the suffering of Jesus on Good Friday to ultimately celebrate his Resurrection on Easter Sunday. With this in mind, I decided to ask students a different question as I came and went from my apartment: "Now that you are fasting from ___, how will you feast?" If fasting is financial, how will you reinvest the money? If it is time or energy, how will you spend the time saved? Because fasting is only one half of the equation. We must also feast.

The focus of a Lean Production System is the reduction of waste. It is a type of fasting. Lean Empowerment is more interested in how we feast once waste is reduced. It is a celebration not of production efficiencies (reduced time/resources/etc.) or financial gains (reduced costs/increased returns), but the greatest opportunity cost of an organization: staff engagement. We can take the experience of reducing waste and the resources saved to reinvest in the very people who helped identify and reduce the waste. We feast on empowerment.

Consider the platitude of the journey and the destination. Mass Production Systems are interested in the destination: Profit. Craft Production Systems are also interested in a destination: Art. In contrast, Lean Production Systems are focused on the journey, not the destination. Focusing attention on the process will have a more prolonged impact on reaching the desired destination than a narrow focus on the goal will ever achieve. But the Lean Empowerment System takes this nuanced approach a step further. It redirects our focus to the **journeyers** more than the **journey** or the **destination**. The people matter most, not as a means to an end, but an end in themselves.

Philosophical Context: The Two Seasons of Lean

There are two seasons in this world: life and death. The buds of springtime find their demise in winter. The dry season quickly turns to the wet season. Cells either expand or decompose. The only constant in life is change, or the alternative is death, so if we aren't changing, then we are dying. In the words of Robert Miller, author of *Hearing the Voice of the Shingo Principles*: "When I stop growing, I start to die."[7]

The work of people also adheres to the law of the seasons. The tension between life and death is often repeated in Lean literature and is expressed in different ways. In its most basic form, we see how each employee has two jobs – to do their work and to improve their work.[8] Masaaki Imai, disciple of the first Lean models in Japan, defines these two jobs as maintenance and Kaizen. Joseph M. Juran, American consultant and founding voice of Lean, defines them as control and breakthrough. Understanding their respective definitions is important to understanding the two seasons of Lean.

Control and Breakthrough (Juran)

According to Juran, "Breakthrough and Control are also part of one continuing cycle of events."[9] "Breakthroughs are called drives, campaigns, programs, breakouts. Control is called firefighting, holding the line, restoring the status quo, staying the course, getting back on target."[10] In other words, breakthrough is the creation of good changes, whereas control is the prevention of bad changes.

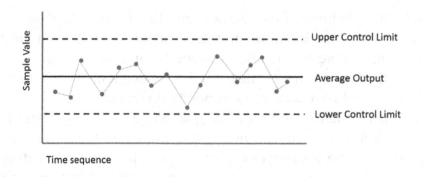

Figure 0.2   General example of control limits.

It is important, for this discussion, to recognize how Juran was deeply influenced by the works of Walter Shewhart, statistical theorist from the early 20th century. Shewhart is most well-known for his introduction of statistical control charts as a method of measuring data that is within the limits of control or outside of the limits of control. A set of control limits is calculated from existing data to understand if future actions are within reasonable limits or worth exploring. (Figure 0.2)

His understanding of the seasons follows suit: the first goal of a system is to stay in control while seeking ways to shift the entire limits of control to an improved level of performance by means of breakthrough.

Maintenance and Kaizen (Improvement) (Imai)

One of the most important decisions in change management is knowing what to conserve when making a change.[11] Change can be a destabilizing process for many people, which makes it especially important for agents of change to highlight both what is changing and what is remaining the same. Mark Graban understood the import role that maintenance plays in the process of improvement: "We need to approach our daily business in two phases. One is to maintain the status quo, in which the standard is established and followed. This process is called maintenance and requires dedicated management effort to sustain it, but it is often overlooked or belittled. The second phase is Kaizen, which means to find a better way and revise the current standard. Thus, maintaining and improving the standard becomes the main task of management."[12]

Work and improvement, the two seasons of Lean, are known for how they appear at their best and their worst. At its best, control/maintenance is responsible for the creation of standards and data in statistical control. At its worst, we overemphasize firefighting and neglect the season of improvement. For some it can become a stagnant state of control seeking instead of improving or breakthrough. On the other hand, breakthrough/kaizen is responsible for rapid experimentation and the shifting of control limits. But at its worst, staff are thrashed around by leaders and their short-term "flavor of the month" programs designed to improve company performance. Leaders "discount the future," thinking only for the short term instead of long term.[13]

Each one of us must be intentional about scheduling time in each season, especially improvement. Some organizations can fluctuate between the two naturally, but many get stuck in the mode of firefighting and risk neglecting improvement. Everyone in a system is responsible for welcoming the season of change. We can start by having a "never-ending dissatisfaction with things the way they are and a powerful drive to constantly be seeking a better way."[14] Unfortunately, many staff hold a common sentiment that they are only responsible for work and not for improvement. This is known by another name, "theory x," which assumes people do not like to work.[15] This dangerous assumption is also the basis for Stereotype Threat Theory, a popular idea in the growing study of habit and identity. According to this theory, we tend to conform to a stereotype when we believe we are in it.[16] Consider a person who believes and tells others how he is "not good with technology." He uses this excuse to avoid any opportunity to use technology, even if it improves his quality of life or connectivity with others. His skills with technology will never improve because his identity is tied to its avoidance. Now consider someone who is training for a 10k race. Her likelihood of finishing the race in record time improves if she refers to herself as a "runner." Accountability and outcomes increase if we "make it till we make it," not just "fake it till we make it." This book assumes that humans are naturally bursting forth with energy, and it is up to us to channel that energy.[17] We must use this energy to learn the seasons of life and death, work and improvement. A new Lean Empowerment System must align with the changes inherent in each season. Only then can we transform our companies and our people.

Experiential Context: Stories

Finally, the Lean Empowerment System must appeal to the experience of real people in the workforce, not just ideals or archetypes. I will introduce fictionalized stories throughout this book, some based on personal experience, and others I have heard, to help illustrate the theories that define the Lean Empowerment System.

The Lean Empowerment System will only thrive if our goal is to change the culture and not merely financial success. We must challenge the common idea in management that, to remain competitive, process innovation is essential. Instead, "effective process innovation can only be achieved if strong climates for initiative and psychological safety exist in the company."[18] This goal is not fully measurable by patient experience scores, staff satisfaction ratings or financial statements. The real results are intangible. We must learn from the organizations who have tried to implement Six Sigma or Lean Production Systems but never realized the promised results.

And improvement takes patience. Stroh, a leading voice in Systems Theory, explains, "most people tend to expect to see improvements faster than they are capable of developing. Expecting the system to shift quickly can lead to unrealistic demands for growth that ultimately slow down if not kill it entirely."[19] Similarly, CEO of ThedaCare, John Toussaint, explained that measuring an ROI from Lean improvement "signals to people that lean is a cost-savings initiative, which is absolutely wrong. Lean is a cultural transformation."[20] Finally, former Chief Innovation Officer (CIO) of Cleveland Clinic, and current CIO of Kettering Health, Thomas Graham MD, states "nothing kills innovation faster than the weight of expectation."[21] Our process improvement teams must not be hindered by the suffocating effects of expectation. Leadership must believe in Lean as a cultural transformation, not the source of an ROI.

Thank you for joining me on this journey of culture transformation. The literary, historical, philosophical, and personal contexts for this book will act as a solid foundation as we develop the theory and understand the practice of a Lean Empowerment System. For the sake of knowledge workers in the 21st century, it is time for Lean to evolve to what it should have always been.

Notes

1 Alfie Kohn, *Punished by Rewards: The Trouble with Gold Stars, Incentive Plans, A's, Praise, and Other Bribes* (Boston, MA: Mariner Books, 1993), 197. Most consultants or managers view well-being and motivation as important "insofar as they contribute to higher productivity for the organization," not in their own right.

2 Amy C. Edmondson, *The Fearless Organization: Creating Psychological Safety in the Workplace for Learning, Innovation, and Growth* (Hoboken, NJ: John Wiley & Sons, 2019), xiii.

3 M. Baer and M. Frese, Innovation Is Not Enough: Climates for Initiative and Psychological Safety, Process Innovations, and Firm Performance. *Journal of Organizational Behavior*, 24.1 (2003): 45–68.

4 W. H. Baker and K. D. Rolfes, *Lean for the Long Term: Sustainment Is a Myth, Transformation Is Reality* (New York, NY: Productivity Press, 2017), 167.
   Michael Ballé and D. T. Jones, *The Lean Sensei: Go See Challenge* (Boston, MA: Lean Enterprise Institute, 2019), 73.

5 Daniel Markovitz, *Building the Fit Organization: Six Core Principles for Making Your Company Stronger, Faster, and More Competitive* (New York: McGraw-Hill Education, 2016), 3.

6 W. H. Baker and K. D. Rolfes, *Lean for the Long Term: Sustainment Is a Myth, Transformation Is Reality* (New York, NY: Productivity Press, 2017), 39.

7 Robert Miller, *Hearing the Voice of the Shingo Principles: Creating Sustainable Cultures of Enterprise Excellence* (Abingdon, Oxfordshire: Routledge, 2018), 109.

8 Thomas P. Huber, et al., Microsystems in Health Care: Part 8. Developing People and Improving Work Life: What Front-Line Staff Told Us. *Joint Commission Journal on Quality and Safety*, 29.10 (2003): 519. doi:10.1016/s1549-3741(03)29061-4

9 Joseph M. Juran, *Managerial Breakthrough: A New Concept of the Manager's Job* (New York, NY: McGraw-Hill, 1964), 6.

10 Ibid., 7.

11 Peter Senge, *The Fifth Discipline* (Manhattan, NY: Random House Business, 2006), 335.

12 Forward by Masaaki Imai in Mark Graban, *Healthcare Kaizen: Engaging Front-Line Staff in Sustainable Continuous Improvements* (Boca Raton, FL: CRC Press, 2018), xxv–xxvi.

13 Amy C. Edmondson, *The Fearless Organization: Creating Psychological Safety in the Workplace for Learning, Innovation, and Growth* (Hoboken, NJ: John Wiley & Sons, 2019), 4.

14 Robert Miller, *Hearing the Voice of the Shingo Principles: Creating Sustainable Cultures of Enterprise Excellence* (Abingdon, Oxfordshire: Routledge, 2018), 103.

15 Daniel Pink, *Drive* (London: Penguin Group, 2011), 74.

16 Timothy R. Clark, *The 4 Stages of Psychological Safety: Defining the Path to Inclusion and Innovation* (Oakland, CA: Berrett-Koehler Publishers, Inc., 2020), 49.

17 Ronald Rolheiser, *The Holy Longing, The Search for a Christian Spirituality* (New York, NY: Image, 2019). And it has been shown that we are more likely to reach flow at work than leisure in Daniel Pink, *Drive* (London, Penguin Group, 2011), 127.

18 M. Baer and M. Frese, Innovation Is Not Enough: Climates for Initiative and Psychological Safety, Process Innovations, and Firm Performance. *Journal of Organizational Behavior*, 24.1, (2003): 63.

19 David Stroh, *Systems Thinking for Social Change: A Practical Guide to Solving Complex Problems, Avoiding Unintended Consequences, and Achieving Lasting Results* (Chelsea, VT: Chelsea Green Publishing, 2015), 48.

20 Emily Adams and John Toussaint, *Management on the Mend: The Healthcare Executive Guide to System Transformation* (Appleton, WI: ThedaCare Center for Healthcare Value, 2015).

21 Thomas Graham, *Innovation the Cleveland Clinic Way: Powering Transformation by Putting Ideas to Work* (New York, NY: McGraw-Hill Education, 2016), 22.

THEORY

I

Chapter 1

The Vices of Production and the Virtues of Empowerment

Virtue and Vice

Virtue and vice form two poles within us, like the Earth on its axis. The soul oscillates between each, stuck in a tension between base animalistic tendencies and a sense of greater purpose. We swing between deficiency and excess, being and nothingness.

Let us borrow the language of virtue and vice from moral philosophy and apply it to organizational design. Much insight will be gained as we travel the interdisciplinary bridge between the two. We must define our natural human inclinations and the cultural forces that hold us back from the organizational transformation that we so deeply desire. Only then, after facing our shortcomings, can we propose a new comprehensive system for Lean. To start, let us define three of the main characteristics of virtue and vice: they are communal terms, they develop gradually, and virtue is the balance between deficiency and excess. After sharing a common language about virtue, we will introduce the Vices of Production and the corresponding Virtues of Empowerment.

Anyone familiar with virtue and vice will immediately think of the Four Cardinal Virtues (Prudence, Justice, Fortitude, and Temperance) and the Three Theological Virtues (Faith, Hope, and Charity [Love]). These directly contrast what have been coined the "Seven Deadly Sins:" Pride, Envy, Sloth, Anger, Covetousness, Gluttony and Lust. Following this trend, The Vices of Production and Virtues of Empowerment provide a common language for us to use as we continue to introduce new ideas throughout the book.

DOI: 10.4324/9781032644134-3   **17**

Virtue and Vice Are Communal Terms

The ideas of virtue and vice were born in the Greek polis (city), a very different setting from our Western society. A comparison of now and then reveals an important point: individualism or egocentrism would have made little sense to those living in the polis. A person's entire life, including her profession and actions, was defined in relation to the community and her impact on others.[1] Virtue and vice, therefore, were not something that individuals could embody outside of their community.[2] They were intrinsically communal terms, not individual traits. We must do our best to define virtue and vice once again in the context of the community or organization in which they arise. They describe a group, not a person.

Virtue and Vice Develop Gradually

Our Western culture of instant gratification does little to accommodate traditional definitions of virtue and vice since the growth of each does not happen overnight. Rather, they grow slower than our ability to recognize them. This abstract idea is clearly illustrated in the history of theological ethics or more specifically the subspecialty of virtue ethics.[3] Pause to consider one popular example from Christian ethics: the temptations of Satan form the seeds of vice in our soul and may eventually lead to sinful actions. But our modern obsession with the consequences of sin makes us miss the most important and most sinister element of vice: a sinful idea is most effective when it is not realized by the person within whom it grows. In other words, a weed thrives when it is hidden.

C.S. Lewis artistically illustrates this idea in his book *The Screwtape Letters*. He imagines the correspondence between two demons who scheme to plant evil thoughts in the soul of a person. Screwtape is the demonic equivalent to a guardian angel who has been assigned to tempt the heart of a Christian. His letters to Wormwood, his superior, describe his progress (or lack thereof). Wormwood urges him, "Our policy, for the moment, is to conceal ourselves...If any faint suspicion of your existence begins to arise in his mind, suggest to him a picture of something in red tights, and persuade him that since he cannot believe in that (it is an old textbook method of confusing them) he therefore cannot believe in you."[4] Distraction buys time for vice to grow unnoticed. Each person on the journey of virtue must remember that the growth of virtue and vice are gradual and are, as a result, often overlooked. It is wise to bring each into the light to avoid unwanted growth or celebrate fulfillment.

Virtue Is the Balance Between Deficiency (Vice) and Excess (Vice)

Aristotle defined virtue as a Golden Mean (average) between the vices of deficiency and excess.[5] We can learn a great deal about human behavior in the workplace when we apply this theory. The first vice, deficiency, stems from the expectation of staff to perform without a system of support from the top. This is commonly packaged as a "hands off" style of management and sometimes improperly under the banner of "empowerment." At its extreme, complete deficiency is rarely visible in an organization because it is an immediate sign of failure. If questioned, no leader would admit "I have no system." Instead, organizations will fabricate processes to address immediate needs. These makeshift processes, which lack clarity or structure, often fail to address any long-term needs to the chagrin of the workforce.

The second vice, excess, is how we define waste in a Lean Production System. We often see them outlined in the acronym DOWNTIME: Defects, Overproduction, Waiting, Non-Utilized Talent, Transportation, Inventory, Motion, and Extra-Processing. Excess among knowledge workers is also visible in micromanagement, the excessive monitoring of remote employees, and unhealthy expectations of work outside of regular business hours. In the end, excess is far easier to recognize than deficiency; if it smells like waste, and looks like waste, it is probably waste.

The Golden Mean (virtue) cannot exist in an organization unless leadership provides appropriate levels of support and guidance from the top. Staff must also feel truly empowered at the front line. Consider the idea of statistical control (Figure 1.1): virtue is data within a range of control whereas vice is variation outside of the control limits. Identifying the variation is the first step toward bringing it back within control.

Virtue and vice must be defined communally, gradually, and as a balance between deficiency and excess. Now, equipped with this basic knowledge, our journey toward virtue can begin.

According to Alasdair MacIntyre, a leading voice in virtue ethics, "The good life for man is the life spent in seeking for the good life for man."[6] The simple act of trying to be virtuous is where virtue is found. We hear this repeated in a commonly cited platitude: "the journey is more important than the destination." Yet through the lens of virtue, we recognize that, although the journey is more important than the destination, there remains yet a more important focus: The people with whom we journey. In a world of mass production focused on the *destination*, or Lean production systems

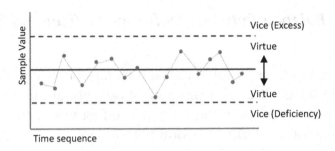

Figure 1.1 Virtue and vice as control limits.

focused on the *journey*, we must develop a Lean empowerment system that is focused on the *journeyers*. It is through and with others that we become virtuous.

We must address the most common vices that limit the transformation of organizational culture before proposing a new comprehensive system for Lean. These can be categorized into the four Vices of Production: **Heroes, Management, Projects, and Burning Platforms**. Our systematic exploration of each vice starts with the identification of a problem, followed by a review of the vice at each end of the spectrum (excess and deficiency). We must understand how each vice manifests itself as both excess and deficiency. The extremes of each vice are resolved by the introduction of a corresponding Virtue of Empowerment (Golden Mean): **Ordinariness, Peer Problem Solving, Kaizen, and Design**.

Vice 1: Hero Dependence

Would the extraordinary actions of a superhero be necessary if the ordinary systems in which they act could handle the problem at hand? We must accept the unpopular opinion that Batman would be unnecessary if the Gotham City Police Department could keep the city safe from villains. This brings us to a base assumption that is critical for the current argument: systems can handle any real-world problem. Although this seems reasonable, stop, and consider the cultural forces that rise against it. The media exaggerates problems to the point of creating supervillains out of daily problems. The more exaggerated the problem, the more we look for solutions outside of the capability of a system. Exaggerations are profitable clickbait that eventually benefit both hero and villain. No publicity is bad publicity. And each villain elicits unpredictable "heroic" behavior among independent actors who may otherwise not act if the system did not

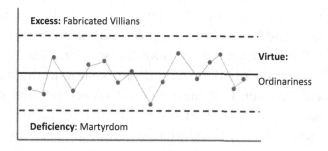

Figure 1.2 Vice 1: Hero dependence.

implicitly encourage it. Villains bring out the best in people but the worst in systems (Figure 1.2).

Our response to heroic actions also adds fuel to the fire. Heroes are celebrated by leaders who, out of good intention, respond to complexity or a problem with the momentary simplicity of heroism. The reliance on heroes can quickly become a vehicle for short-term solutions that drain resources which could instead be invested in Root Cause Analysis or more sustainable solutions. But celebrating heroism is the easiest and most culturally acceptable way for a leader to deflect attention away from an issue. Nobody will argue with an award ceremony. It is a deeply ingrained cultural artifact.

Excess: Fabricated Villains

Hero recognition begets heroic actions. This forms a cycle that can trap individual heroic actors outside of a system while devaluing the steady and ordinary actors in a system. And, once recognized, a hero will continue to make heroic actions to retain their status of "hero." When one villain is overcome, the hero will seek out new opportunities to act heroic, sometimes exaggerating or fabricating potential villains for the sake of triumph. This vicious cycle traps both the hero and those who are inspired by heroic actions.

The broken system also anticipates the hero to produce heroic results. In the language of statistical control theory, a single variation may help a system reach a new range of statistical control, but it is more often an extreme circumstance or momentary blip. Heroic recognition encourages variation, which is antithetical to the formation of a stable system. The hero is at risk of becoming a variant by definition.

Witnesses to the variation will experience a similar cycle to the hero, but the investment is hope instead of pride. The initial onslaught of recognition given to the hero creates a shared hopefulness about the situation in everyone around. But, as the hero seeks out more opportunities to act heroic, it is inevitable that the hero will fail without the support of a stable system. She will seek the next destination instead of dwelling in the journey and those on the road with her. Repeated failure to reach another destination exposes the variant and the broken system, which germinates seeds of hopelessness in the hearts of bystanders where hope once lived. The has-been-hero eventually gives up on both the destination and the journey, and instead reminisces on the dream of heroism that once brought her recognition. In the end, the improvement process stalls as bystanders wait for the next hit of heroism to regain hope and bring us back to where we started.

Deficiency: Martyrdom

Heroes deserve to not be heroes. They deserve a system that lets them excel without everyone relying on them. For example, I once heard a story about a woman who received an award for her clinical role in administering vaccines during the COVID-19 pandemic. After the award ceremony an attendee remarked to her, "you're crushing it!" to which she responded "Thanks… crushing it…and getting crushed *by* it."

Heroes are quickly martyred by the broken systems that recognize them. For example, many essential workers were expected to be martyrs for the common good during the COVID-19 pandemic. Teachers were expected to teach their previous curricula in a new remote setting with little preparation. Then, as in-person classes returned, they were expected to split their energy and continue offering remote opportunities for students who were uncomfortable joining in person. Nurses were also expected to pick up the slack during the nursing shortage caused by burnout or sickness. Float requests became mandatory as nurses became patients. Extraordinary efforts were heralded as heroic, but compensation remained unchanged, and systems unaltered. We cannot be surprised to hear that these heroes went from the valiant subjects of billboards, yard signs, and etched glass statues to travel nurses who are gaming the very system that celebrated them.

Virtue: Ordinariness

It is easy to notice that people in the business world love heroes, so how do we remove the negative outcomes without sacrificing the positive?[7] There is an important distinction in theology between transformation and reformation that can be applied here. Reformation refers to the simple shifting of existing pieces to create new things. Breakthroughs are even defined as re-combinations of new or existing knowledge to make a new solution.[8] On the other hand, transformation takes the same elements and alters them to serve a new purpose, often changing their intrinsic nature. The heroic elements of recognition, hope, and innovation are worth retaining outside of the structure of heroism, but they must undergo transformation to serve a new purpose: a system of ordinary people. This is only possible by rewarding laziness, devaluing "hard work," and removing the underbrush.

Reward Laziness

Bill Gates is often attributed with the saying, "I choose a lazy person to do a hard job. Because a lazy person will find an easy way to do it."[9] This suggests a shift from the work ethic that permeates the Western world. It honors and celebrates the ordinary person who avoids unnecessary work (waste) that distracts from value-added parts of life. But we must not mistake laziness with apathy or avoidance of work. Instead, let us understand laziness as a repulsion of waste. Organizations must learn how to observe laziness as untapped potential energy instead of a source of negative kinetic energy.

Lazy employees have fostered a bias, one that is often true, that their work is not value-added to the customer or the process. As a result, they are the least likely to act heroic. But the ordinary steps they take out of laziness can lead to profound process improvements that redirect the focus back to the customer. Imagine a desk receptionist at a dental office. She spends an average of thirteen seconds checking in patients compared to a network average of ninety seconds across the other regional locations. Upon further observation, this worker found that she was able to confirm many check-in steps during the pre-registration process before the patient arrived, a process which had been encouraged by leadership but rarely adopted over the past few years. When asked why she followed this process, the staff member explained that their office had been a staple in the community for a long time and they know all their patients by name. After they were acquired by the parent organization, they were asked to follow new processes, which often distracted her from connecting with patients in the waiting room. The pre-registration process allowed her to be lazy when the patient arrived and simply chat with them as they waited for the hygienist. Her desire to chat with patients and make the day go faster led to some of the highest patient experience scores around.

Devalue "Hard Work"

The term "hard worker," once a staple in résumés and interviews, should be considered a warning sign for employers. A hard worker acts with brute force. She measures her time and effort in terms of capacity, fitting more work into the same forty hours to appear more productive than others, with little interest in efficiency or prudence. The purpose or value of the work itself is secondary to the work ethic.

The heroic hard worker is an artifact from an era when most of the work was non-knowledge work. Our contemporary setting is different. The phrase "knowledge work" was only coined in the late 1950s by famous business consultant, Peter Drucker, which illustrates a pivot in the role and expectations of the average American worker.[10] The typical organization began looking at every employee as a knowledge worker, regardless of their role or job duties. It is now critical to accept that all work is knowledge work.[11] This is based in the two seasons of Lean: do work and improve work.

The title of "hard worker" remains a cultural golden calf despite its consistent misapplication to the average knowledge worker. It is clearly visible in a Cadillac commercial from 2014, which follows a businessman as he reflects on the American work ethic.[12] The actor walks from his backyard pool through an elegant house to a new Cadillac in his driveway. He asks, "Why aren't we like [other countries]? Because we are crazy driven hard-working believers, that's why." He goes on to cite a few common household names, including the Wright Brothers, Les Paul, and Ali, as examples of hard workers to be imitated. The commercial closes with the statement: "It's pretty simple: you work hard, you create your own luck, and you got to believe anything is possible."[13] Sound familiar?

Hard workers hide behind the American work ethic, which is based on an argumentative fallacy of "on principle." A person who argues "on principle" will shift the argument from the truth of the topic to the merit of the content. Think about the last argument you witnessed when one party ceased to argue from their original premise and instead shifted to say, "I don't care about that anymore; it's just the principle that matters." This fallacy is invoked in the absence of strong evidence when the defendant wants to protect a remnant of the past rather than focusing on the current truth. The American work ethic is the perfect example for an argument "on principle." And the identity of a hard worker is threatened by systems that encourage efficiency, so they are held at arms-length with deep skepticism. Administrators often assume it is only the apathetic or disengaged staff who oppose organizational change, but they often overlook those who have made a reputation from the very work ethic that spurns progress. Unfortunately, the prevailing notion of "hard work" is so deeply entrenched in organizational culture and politics. It must be challenged by the virtue of ordinariness.

An ordinary worker, unlike the hard worker, has a primal understanding of throughput. She measures success in terms of free time and efficiency (recall the importance of laziness defined above). The popular notion of hard work is less important than the process or the people that help one achieve the desired goal. And what is perceived by onlookers may appear to be hard work, but not for its own sake. It has been transformed toward a new end.

Accepting the countercultural virtue of ordinariness means recognizing the common human quality of laziness. It means celebrating the desire for less work. The role of management is to encourage staff to find an easier method than brute force to produce higher quality results without maximizing capacity. The very people who were less valued in the organizations fixated on the American work ethic are the greatest asset in a company which values ordinariness. More people need to act systematically and avoid heroic gestures. And these leaders will naturally arise among the ordinary staff, not as *extra*ordinary (extra as a prefix meaning "outside the normal course of events"), but *extra*-ordinary, exhibiting ordinary qualities all the time in small ways.[14] St. Mother Teresa of Calcutta is attributed with the phrase, "We cannot all do great things. But we can do small things with great love." This is echoed by St. Therese of Lisieux in her famous "Little Way" to become a saint: "To do small things with great love." The ordinary worker, just like the holy women listed here, is an example for knowledge workers to follow in our modern age.[15]

Remove the Underbrush

According to the book on Shingo Principles: "If we value heroic fire fighters more than quiet individuals and teams… you will always have fires and fire fighters. If we value never-ending continuous improvement by every single person, every single day in every part of the organization, we will eventually clear out the underbrush and debris such that no fuel remains from which a fire can start."[16] The American work ethic rarely celebrates the person who picks up one stick each day. Instead, we celebrate the person who puts out the fire caused by the sticks. In Richard Powers' novel *The Overstory*, protagonist Douglas Pavlicek spends years planting Douglas fir seedlings by hand in response to the rapid deforestation in Oregon. After planting his 50 thousandth seedling, he realizes that his efforts to reduce deforestation are providing the very fuel for future deforestation: new trees. Discouraged and angry, Douglas joins an environmental group that commits arson on logging equipment, which eventually sends him to prison. Douglas' efforts to improve the Earth's biome were not valued by the consumer culture that allowed logging companies to enter protected forests. His efforts were exploited, and he lashed out.

We must be careful not to exploit ordinariness like we have commercialized heroism. Instead, we must reward laziness, devalue "hard work," and deprioritize firefighting in favor of prevention. We must reorient our way of thinking and resist the magnetic pull of prevailing cultural beliefs. Even the slightest disassociation with hero dependence should be celebrated. It is one step toward breaking a vicious cycle that traps many organizations and leaders alike.

Vice 2: Management Dependence

Staff can only succeed in a system that is set up for success. The rest is outside of their control. According to Edwards Deming, Lean pioneer in Japan and the United States, 94% of troubles belong to the system. In his words, "no amount of care or skill in workmanship can overcome fundamental faults in the system."[17] This means a meager 6% of problems are the result of special causes, such as tensions between individual staff members, environmental issues, or acts of God.[18] When confronted by these issues, each one of us is forced to ask, "what is *actually* within my sphere of influence?"

The system is the responsibility of management. And management has a duty to create a system where staff can succeed. But many organizations hold onto the idea that staff have the power to improve a system. For example, during initial process observations it is common to hear the sentiment, "if only (enter name here) worked harder…" or "if only (enter name here) did x, y, z…." then the process wouldn't be an issue. Both staff and managers assume that a process problem can be tied back to the performance of an individual. We continue to place our bets on a losing system. But it is unfair to ask frontline staff to fix a system that is out of their control. This only leaves a 6% likelihood of success. Leaders shouldn't start by blaming a person. Organizations must instead challenge management to refocus attention on their real responsibility: the system.

A systematic solution starts with the diagnosis of a systemic problem. Consider the two types of problems in the healthcare arena: "chronic" and "sporadic" (think acute). Providers must use different strategies to deal with each. Sporadic (acute) deficiencies in health can be handled immediately with little systematic intervention. A broken bone can be fixed with surgery followed with minimal intervention or lifestyle change. Cancer, on the other hand, is not so straightforward. In the words of Juran, improvement strategies that overlook the system and rely on staff are "not a suitable means for dealing with chronic problems."[19] These health conditions, such as back pain, cancer, cardiovascular disease, chronic obstructive pulmonary disease (COPD), or diabetes, are multi-faceted, and require a systematic change of behavior, medication, and care to manage effectively. Management of chronic health conditions requires a care team of providers from multiple specialties. The patient alone cannot be the source of healing.

Doctors must not mistake chronic conditions for acute conditions; neither should management mistake problems in the workforce with systemic problems.

The responsibilities of leaders and staff can be further refined, respectively, as process capability and process performance. Capability is the responsibility of management and performance is the responsibility of staff. Juran defines process capability as "the inherent ability of the process." Process performance "is the actual result achieved." Unfortunately, the process performance often falls short of the inherent ability that is allowed by the capability.[20] Womack, in his famous book *The Machine that Changed the World*, gives us another definition of capability: "manufacturability."[21] No matter the language we use, it is up to leadership to ask if staff are set up for failure or success. Leaders must remember that, if you're thirsty, you are already dehydrated. If staff complain about the system, their success was limited long ago.

Let us review what management dependence looks like at both extremes of vice (Figure 1.3). At the one extreme, managers take the burden from staff to keep the process moving. At the other end, staff sneak around management and conduct improvements to transform an organization. Neither is healthy for the long-term health of an organization.

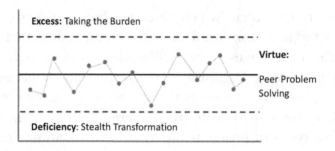

Figure 1.3 Vice 2: Management dependence.

Excess: *Taking the Burden*

Francis was in his first few months as Director of Operations for an outpatient spine center. He was tasked with a long-term process improvement project to reduce check-in time from 8.5 minutes to 7.5 minutes while keeping patient satisfaction scores in the top decile. He observed how the department did not have enough registration staff during the busiest time of day to handle the influx of patients, which ought to have resulted in longer check-in times. Yet, as he explored the data, he found the times were better during this hour than the rest of the day. Did staff experience a rush of adrenaline to do double the work in half the time? No, he learned. The former director admitted to pulling schedulers and coders from the back office to help with registration during this high time, and even worked the desk herself to fix the problem. Everyone was willing to lend a hand, and they claimed that "it worked."

The data did not lie, and nobody complained, but the real problem was effectively invisible. He decided to run an experiment: let the process run its course for a full day to see the real check-in times. The result was instantaneous: staff freaked out. He pulled the band aid off for a minute, and the staff remembered the problem. The director, with the involvement of his team, went on to implement simple and sustainable solutions, which included staggering provider schedules and reducing staff travel times, to effectively reduce the average check-in time to 6.5 minutes. A manager or coder hasn't sat at the front desk since.

Many leaders will defend the choice to come to the aid of staff and take on the burden themselves out of compassion. But their assistance in the field may cause more harm than good. Short-term solutions can become a ·band aid that is forgotten beneath clothing, covering a real problem.

Staff are given a false sense of security and managers are effectively wasting time that could be spent on the process only they can fix: the system. Special causes (6% of their work) distract managers from systematic problems (94% of their work). Although it may be painful, **management must not mistake taking the burden with sharing the burden**.

Taking the burden from staff has the potential to be worse than micromanagement. It fosters an unhealthy codependence, making staff reliant on the leader not only for system design but also for the work in the system. The leader leaves nothing to the ownership of the frontline. And, like hero dependence, it is hard to dispute. It develops gradually when unchallenged. Empowerment is delayed in the name of necessity. And staff will rarely argue against receiving the momentary help they need. Alternatively, micromanagement keeps the work in the hands of staff but with an oppressive level of supervision. It is easier to identify and is less tolerated by organizational culture, making it a quick target for change.

Deficiency: Stealth Transformation

Frontline staff should not feel like they are sneaking around when trying to improve a process. Peter Senge calls this "stealth transformation," a means of shifting an organization in the direction of change when universal support is lacking or minimal.[22] He casts it in a positive light, saying the intent of stealth transformation is not to undermine or go behind the back of leadership. Rather, it is a systematized way of nudging leadership to keep pace with the level of change desired by the frontline. According to Senge, leadership will be willing to come along on the journey if the pace of change is subtle and non-threatening because it is hard to argue with growth. The pace of change is gradual, yet exponential.

Stealth transformation is common in systems where management dependence has been replaced by widespread skepticism of management to bring about change. Staff recite the mantra, "if they won't do it, we will." The frontline quickly learns the art of kaizen (rapid improvement) and, to remain hidden, avoids the theatrics of innovation, but at the cost of eventual chaos.[23] Leadership will eventually catch on to the changes and their distrust will grow. The opportunity for staff to receive the education or mentorship they need will move further out of reach. Empowerment is impossible in a system where staff and leaders are not, in some way, connected.

Virtue: Peer Problem Solving[24]

Different types of change must happen at different levels of an organization. Consider the United States of America. The fifty states have local and state governments in addition to the national systems of governance. The tension of local versus national governance is one of the oldest and core ideologies that separates traditional Democrats from Republicans. Republicans argue that America is a Democratic *Republic*, comprised of fifty different states that require fifty different systems under one unifying set of principles. Subsidiarity, or the assignment of power to the smallest or most local level, is the ruling philosophy of the Republican Party. This starts at the smallest unit, the family, and expands to the city (schools, parks, utilities, etc.) and eventually to the state. When one level fails, the next steps in to subsidize growth and support. The United States Council of Catholic Bishops (USCCB) defends subsidiarity by focusing resources into the house, defined as the "local church," then local churches, and finally the Diocese or Archdiocese. The nature of human relationships is organically self-organizing, but risks corruption without the proper checks and balances.

The idea of change needing to come from the top or macro level is a political philosophy associated with formal Democratic thought. Here, the *Democratic* Republic steps in when the local levels have failed to adequately address the needs of its people. The unifying power of top-down decision-making can be invaluable in response to large-scale catastrophes or the quick mobilization of resources. It can also become susceptible to overreaching or stalling on important decisions by making leaders jump through bureaucratic hoops.

Both subsidiarity and top-down support are appropriate in certain circumstances, but a system must start with subsidiarity. Local teams are the first line of defense, and top-down support should only be tapped when all local options have been exhausted or basic human rights are threatened.

It is important to break free from the assumption that leadership support is always required for change and instead apply the concept of subsidiarity to organizational politics. The team, like the family unit, is the smallest workstream, then the department, and finally the organization. The waste of motion is visible when decision-making moves away from the team closest to the work.[25] When possible, decision-making should remain at the workstream level unless the issue becomes pervasive.

Many traditional approaches in both organizational and political programs assume a *vertical* flow of support: top-down or bottom-up. Since both have shortcomings, it is valuable to propose a new model of *horizontal* support: peer-to-peer problem solving.

Put yourself in the shoes of an executive leader over a restaurant chain with one hundred locations. You have received an influx of recent complaints from local managers about the unrealistic expectations of solving all the problems that arise daily. Burnout is increasing, and some are threatening to leave. How do you respond? A company of this size is simply too large for an executive leader to micromanage frontline staff or intervene locally. Instead, a leader must leverage the knowledge and expertise of peers to help each other. She must become a multiplier.

The presence of Lateral Leaders can relieve the pressure of cross-functional managers to be experts in all things.[26] The role of managers in a Lean Empowerment System, which prefers Lateral Leadership to formal management, is "a support role."[27] Many managers with a traditional view of management may push back against this ideology, but those who adopt modern views of empowerment can share the burden of basic questions to peers instead of taking every burden on themselves. And the time gained can be invested in building systems, supporting people, and creating strategic changes for the whole team. This is the *true work* of management.

Vice 3: Project Dependence

Humans love projects. They are responsible for cell phones, the Internet, and any technology, artwork, or book you can imagine. They are vehicles that move teams of people from point A to point B, progressing an idea toward its manifestation in the world. Each project is deemed a success or a failure based on three criteria: on time, on budget, and on scope. Project Managers follow the standards set forth by the Project Management Institute (PMI) and share a common language of terms like stakeholder management, work breakdown structure, risk analysis, and project plan. It is a highly technical role with more claimants than trained professionals.

Leaders in a Western organization believe that projects are the best (and sometimes *only*) means of making change. Anything smaller in scope is called operational work to be managed locally. Anything larger is a program or portfolio, the mezzo and macro categories of project management. But this dependence has limitations. In excess, organizations become obsessed with big changes, or megalomania. Only the most innovative or out of the box ideas are worth considering. In the opposite direction, deficiency,

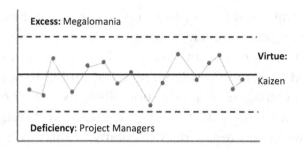

Figure 1.4 Vice 3: Project dependence.

organizational change is limited by the number of project managers on payroll (Figure 1.4). Neither of these extremes can effectively address the pace of change that is required on the frontline.

Excess: Megalomania

Our love for projects is both cultural and rooted in human nature. As a member of Western, and more specifically American culture, I am fully aware of the social messages (influenced by capitalism) to acquire more things and to find the biggest things available. Our dream is to have a big home, with a big truck, where we cook big steaks on our big fancy grill. The motto of Texas is "everything is bigger in Texas," where big achievements and big things are met with big praise. The bigger the better! This is megalomania.

Our obsession with bigness also bleeds into the workplace. We tackle big problems with big projects, seeking massive cost savings and time savings to get big attention and the big promotion. And who leads these big projects? Big heroes! The project managers who juggle hundreds of tasks, manage dozens of stakeholders, and give multi-page status updates are lauded as they cross the finish line and launch the next big product or change for the company.

Human nature also predisposes us toward projects. Imagine crossing off the final task on a project plan or cutting a ribbon at the opening of a new hospital that will serve thousands of new patients. People feel a natural rush of accomplishment when they see an idea to its completion. Home renovation projects are a great example of smaller projects that elicit a similar feeling. I once sat on the floor of my mudroom, after weeks of gradual renovation, to appreciate how each detail of planning came together into a single unified product that serves many purposes. Projects are naturally glamorous, and they elicit a strong emotional response that can border on awe.

Western culture is enamored by the heroic project manager, and human nature is predisposed to the serotonin rush of project completion. Both culture and our human nature are less interested in the team and small experimentation. This innate dependence on projects must be challenged to make way for a much less exciting but much more effective means of completing work.

Deficiency: Project Managers

The improvements prioritized by leadership, such as the reduction of referral leakage or hospital length of stay, can consume an entire resource. Project managers must learn workflows that cross dozens of departments, each with their own unique processes and standards. They juggle hundreds of lead measures that somehow correlate with the desired lag outcome. And ultimately, as a result, the number of improvements an organization can make becomes limited by the number of project managers it can hire.

The dependence of an improvement model on a few charismatic project managers has inherent risk. Recall Craft Production, which relies on a single staff member to design, build, and test a product. Atul Gawande, in his book *Checklist Manifesto* defines this individual as the "Master Builder."[28] The appointment of a master builder injects risk into a system since, in the absence of the builder, a process or project may fall apart. The energy behind a change can start with the passion of an individual but will only be sustained if it transitions into a system that continues the process. A system that relies on the energy of a single person is not a system; it is a straw house.

Project managers are hired before process engineers are even considered because Lean and Six Sigma, the two dominant improvement methodologies, depend on charismatic facilitators to garner support, lead value mapping sessions, go to the Gemba, and hold teams accountable, to name a few.[29] They are treated as projects, and the size and scope of such initiatives often require a leader who aligns more with project management expertise than process engineers mentioned in Japanese literature. Any improvement model risks becoming yet another project when it is treated as one instead of a cultural transformation. Miller, in his book *Hearing the Voice of the Shingo Principles*, expresses this concern: "I hear so many people today talk about efforts to build continuous improvement into their culture largely by creating better programs, hiring better consultants, requiring top management participation at key events, etc. But, even knowing how hard it is to really and fundamentally change culture, more cultural improvement efforts become 'programs' themselves and eventually fail for the same reasons as the continuous improvement events."[30]

Virtue: Kaizen

There are two types of improvement: continuous improvement and discontinuous improvement. Discontinuous improvement is defined by project-led changes. It is the very problem this section has sought to address. According to Hines and Butterworth, companies in the early stage of enterprise improvement "tend to rely (too) heavily on discontinuous improvement."[31] The "move towards spending more time on identifying and implementing the smaller continuous improvement activities tends to occur as organizations mature."[32]

Continuous improvement borrows the language of experimentation from scientific theory. And it is more commonly known as "Kaizen," which will be defined in detail in Chapter 6. Kaizen is illustrated well in the Japanese saying, "One step forward by 100 people is better than 100 steps by a single person."[33] Its success is traditionally measured in the volume of ideas, not their magnitude. Most importantly, it requires the input and engagement of the frontline to identify changes that directly impact their work. Their ideas may be small or the outcome boring, but each improvement signals to the frontline that their voice is heard, and the system works. And projects still have a place, but do not take up all the space.

Now, imagine an empty jar, and pour in a handful of rocks.[34] Only so many can fit, and there is visibly wasted space between each one. These stones represent large discontinuous improvement projects managed by a few project managers. Now, drop in as many pebbles as you can; they fill the gaps between the rocks and reduce the wasted space. Each pebble is an average sized initiative such as a Six Sigma Event, PDCA, cross-functional improvement, single patient value stream, or A3. Finally, pour a cup of sand into the jar. All remaining gaps are filled, keeping the stones and pebbles from jostling around. The grains of sand signify daily kaizen at the frontline. Each organization must determine their own ratio of stones to pebbles to sand. We must end our dependence on massive discontinuous improvements that require project managers and consider the other forms of continuous improvement. All three are necessary for a cultural transformation.

Vice 4: Urgency Dependence

I once heard a division President say, "Don't waste a good emergency." In the matter of a week, this simple statement was the guiding light for thousands of healthcare organizations across the country. Everyone clamored to launch Telehealth platforms in a matter of days after slowly testing products for years. What was the emergency that caused such a dramatic change? The COVID-19 pandemic. Companies put on hold any previously defined strategy or independent team goal as leaders congregated in conference rooms and command centers to focus on the one shared problem. Dozens of reactive strategies were quickly identified with corresponding action plans written in a matter of hours. Businesses proved that the speed of change can truly bypass the slog of political bureaucracy. Years of evolution happened in weeks.

But what happens when an emergency is no longer an emergency? What happens when the hospital census drops? It is easy to discuss strategy when a company has a common enemy, and the goal is clearly defined. It is easy to act quickly when our platform is burning. But when a fire starts to wane, leaders no longer know where to stand. Teams will slowly return to their usual operations and individual projects, with varied levels of alignment and prioritization. Without a new burning platform, we choose our own next step. In the words of Toussaint, "without a burning platform to create clarity and urgency, most people are happy to agree that change is needed – elsewhere."[35]

Organizations learned that their leaders would create their own structure in the absence of strategy. They tasted the power of urgency, and some sought to recreate it. Not as another burning platform, playing hopscotch from strategy to strategy, but unified behind a core framework. There is a common belief among leaders that a crisis is required to instill lasting change. This idea is reiterated by many Lean leaders, including Womack,[36] Toussaint,[37] and other contemporary sources.[38] But the past few years sparked an enlightened and unpopular response voiced by many teams in the post-pandemic era: The power of an emergency is unmistakable, but it is unsustainable. Urgency is a vice that must be tempered by the virtue of design (Figure 1.5).

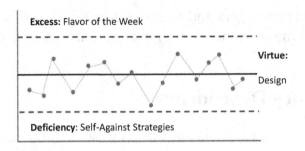

Figure 1.5 Vice 4: Urgency dependence.

Excess: *Flavor of the Week*

A burning platform can help garner leadership support, but it also risks becoming a "flavor of the week." On one hand, we observe Lean consultants who create a rallying cry to pit an organization against a dire need to win the support of leadership. Inspirational speakers or interdepartmental marketing can band many different cross-functional teams around a meaningful idea. We see these same tactics used in political marketing during wartime or election cycles to spark action and gain support from voters.[39]

On the other hand, leadership can quickly pivot their attention to a different burning platform based on any number of factors. New pressures from leadership, exciting opportunities for growth, or simple distractions can quickly grow into the next important "flavor of the week" that reaps the attention, energy, and resources of an organization. The excitement of frequently changing priorities can cause whiplash for team members, eventually leading to distrust, disengagement, or turnover.

And the impacts are not limited to psychological distrust. Remnants of unchallenged waste are also carried over from one "flavor of the week" into the next. For example, staff make concessions for each burning platform and accommodate extra work as "necessary evils" that should one day be replaced by a better process.[40] They are given assurances that the additional work in the short term will pave the way to better outcomes or more efficient processes in the long term. Unfortunately, instead of staying to invest in the current process, leaders jump to a different burning platform and fail to remove the waste that was implemented for the previous platform. Remnants of waste become the standards of the next system.

Deficiency: Self-Against Strategies

A political advertisement is defined as "negative" if it contains an attack or contrast with the rival political candidate. According to a study by the Wesleyan Media Project, the volume of negative advertisements increased by 61% over the 2014 midterms.[41] The sudden spike in negative attack or contrast strategies instead of positive strategies has a deep philosophical implication for politics. One that also applies to organizational strategy. The question must be posed: "Is it better to define yourself as yourself, or define yourself against someone or something else?"

At its best, the definition of a group against a burning platform or urgent situation can band people together against a shared injustice, environmental disaster, or medical pandemic. At its worst, it can manifest in very destructive movements, including (but not limited to) antisemitism, apartheid, and systemic racism. Patterns of fear and self-protection underlie decisions throughout history to choose violence. In the end, negativity is often chosen because it is easier to define our **self-against** a burning platform than reflect on how we would define our **self-for**.[42] Aspiration and introspection takes time. Hatred doesn't.

Groups who are defined as self-against have a disadvantage to groups who are defined as self-for. Imagine a Research and Development (R&D) division within a larger organization. Each year the team plans an offsite strategic planning retreat to define divisional goals for the upcoming year. But, as the day of the retreat loomed, the leaders grew increasingly jaded about the session. Some considered taking the day off or extending weekend plans. All of them dreaded a single and inevitable conversation about identity. Their division had always been defined in the shadow of the parent organization. Executive leaders were left out of meetings, placed at the end of agendas, or received frequent budget cuts. The tension had reached a breaking point and tainted many conversions. But the division president, hopeful for a breakthrough, convinced his team to attend.

On the day of the retreat, the team wrestled about whether they could define themselves as a unique department or continue defining themselves in the shadow of the parent organization. The facilitator posed a challenge: "What is keeping you from defining your own goals?" The only reason the executive leaders could think of was the fear of the parent organization seeing their strategy of self-for as a political move against the group or a strategic power-grab. But after hours of discussion, the executive leaders ultimately decided it was time to shift the definition from self-against to self-for. Clarity was worth the risk.

Surprisingly enough, the team's self-for definition was not once challenged by the parent organization as they feared. It was even adopted within the global strategy of the parent organization! As a result, the R&D department and all its employees, from the executive team to the frontline, have experienced a deep sense of meaning, purpose, and clarity. They learned that, at its core, a strategy cannot be a definition of self-against. Strategy must be defined as self-for.

Virtue: Design

Leaders must have somewhere else to go if they step off a burning platform. This requires the designing of a space that isn't on fire. According to Senge, "The hallmark of good design is the absence of crisis."[43] Let us learn how to make this leap out of urgency and into design. (In Chapter 4 we will take a deep dive into the topic of Systems Thinking and review system models. Here we can at least gain a preliminary understanding of the importance of system design and its impact on an organization.)

According to Lean pioneer, Mark Graban, "Pain and possibilities are the 2 parents of transformation." These parents teach us to dream of what is possible, while at the same time reminding us of the pain that can result if we do not improve.[44] We can learn the hard way, through repeated failure, or the easy way, through education and mentorship. Put another way, "offensive innovation" is us choosing to change, whereas "defensive innovation" is change choosing us.[45] The theme of the two seasons in the Introduction of this book continues to unfold as we live in the tension between preparation and reaction, design and urgency.

Leaders must be designers of systems, both for themselves and their staff.[46] Those who fail to design systems will resemble Sisyphus, eternally pushing a boulder up a hill to see it roll back to the bottom.[47] The same leaders wonder why all their efforts are ineffective or unsustainable. But recent motivational theories propose that leaders cannot motivate; all they can do is create a system that encourages improvement and removes barriers.[48] Motivation is an internal process that thrives on clarity and is defined as self-for instead of self-against. It is rooted in purpose and meaning, not the fleeting excitement of the next burning platform or "flavor of the week." And our staff, without a properly designed system, will resemble a boat crew at sea with a poorly designed rudder: spinning in circles, caught between crosswinds, and occasionally knocked overboard by a swinging boom. Recall the vice of management dependence: staff perform the best they can in their circumstances. Leaders and staff alike must hardcode quality at the design phase.[49]

Design allows us to react gracefully when the need arises. No amount of design, or the decision to change, can prepare us for every possible situation. Some reaction will be required, but the benefits of design will carry over into these moments. We become free to react with strategic direction and a general sense of compassion instead of thrashing between disruptions. (We will continue to explore the ideas of self-induced chaos and personal work management as personal manifestations of urgency dependence in Chapter 6.)

Organizations cannot wait around for a burning platform or a sense of urgency to change. Design a system instead. Go on that diet because it is the right thing to do, not the only way out. If you throw spaghetti at a wall, you might as well cover it in plates. And be wary of any strategy that steals the title of a book. Only then can you avoid the common perception that Lean is another "flavor of the week" or burning platform.

This chapter is a hermeneutic lens – based on the four Vices of Production and their respective Virtues of Empowerment – through which you can study any improvement methodology. Our dependence on heroes, management, projects, and urgency holds us back from real transformation. Only by celebrating ordinariness, peer problem solving, Kaizen, and design can we hope to shift a culture from production to empowerment.

Before you try to apply the four Virtues of Empowerment to your work, we must practice! The next chapter is a training ground where we can analyze three artifacts of Lean Production that are commonly implemented in companies and discussed in Lean literature. Only after we critically evaluate and learn lessons from these ideas can we propose a comprehensive Lean Empowerment System to take its place in the evolutionary cycle.

Notes

1 We also see this in the modern idea of "teaming" which argues for a return to the communal way of thinking in Amy C. Edmondson, *The Fearless Organization: Creating Psychological Safety in the Workplace for Learning, Innovation, and Growth* (Hoboken, NJ: John Wiley & Sons, 2019), xiv.

2 This introduces two novel ideas in Western society: systemic virtue and systemic vice. (We will pick back up on this idea in Chapter 4 on Systems Theory.)

3 Peter Senge, *The Fifth Discipline* (Manhattan, NY: Random House Business, 2006), 123.

4 C.S. Lewis, *The Screwtape Letters* (New York, NY: HarperCollins Publishers, 2012).

5 Borrowed from Character Strengths and Virtues (CSV) (contemporary): https://en.wikipedia.org/wiki/Character_Strengths_and_Virtues.

6 Alasdair MacIntyre, *After Virtue: A Study in Moral Theology* (Notre Dame, IN: University of Notre Dame Press, 1984), 219.

7 Peter Senge, *The Fifth Discipline* (Manhattan, NY: Random House Business, 2006), 40.

8 Timothy R. Clark, *The 4 Stages of Psychological Safety: Defining the Path to Inclusion and Innovation* (Oakland, CA: Berrett-Koehler Publishers, Inc., 2020), 109.

9 Many people argue that Gates did not actually make this statement since the sentiment can be found in literature and politics since the 1920s.

10 https://www.forbes.com/sites/forbestechcouncil/2020/12/10/the-year-of-the-knowledge-worker/?sh=998a5377fbba

11 Timothy R. Clark, *The 4 Stages of Psychological Safety: Defining the Path to Inclusion and Innovation* (Oakland, CA: Berrett-Koehler Publishers, Inc., 2020), 58.

12 I will use the term "American Work Ethic" to refer to the modern reflection of the Protestant Work Ethic that has developed uniquely in the United States. This is a meritocracy based on pop-behaviorism.

13 Cadillac – "Poolside" – 2014. https://www.youtube.com/watch?v=gTRj-fp-bP0

14 https://www.etymonline.com/word/extraordinary

15 Patrick Graupp and Martha Purrier, *Getting to Standard Work in Health Care: Using TWI to Create a Foundation for Quality Care.* (New York, NY: Productivity Press, 2022).

16 Robert Miller, *Hearing the Voice of the Shingo Principles: Creating Sustainable Cultures of Enterprise Excellence* (Abingdon, Oxfordshire: Routledge, 2018), 105.

17 W. Edwards Deming, *The New Economics: For Industry, Government, Education* (Cambridge, MA: The MIT Press, 2018), 33.

18 W. Edwards Deming, *Out of the Crisis* (Cambridge, MA: The MIT Press, 2018), 315.

19 J. M. Juran, *Juran on Leadership for Quality: An Executive Handbook* (Florence, MA: Free Press, 1989), 168.

20 Ibid., 125.

21 James Womack, Daniel Jones, and Daniel Roos, *The Machine that Changed the World* (Manhattan, NY: Simon & Schuster, 2007), 96–97.

22 Ibid., 298.

23 Masaaki Imai, *Kaizen (ky'zen): The Key to Japan's Competitive Success* (New York City, NY: McGraw-Hill, 1991), 23.

24 This section is a purposefully abridged introduction to the idea of Lateral Leaders which demands its own chapter (Chapter 5 – People).

25 Similarly, psychological safety lives at the group level in an organization, not the entire organization in Amy C. Edmondson, *The Fearless Organization: Creating Psychological Safety in the Workplace for Learning, Innovation, and Growth* (Hoboken, NJ: John Wiley & Sons, 2019), 11.

26 Masaaki Imai, *Kaizen (ky'zen): The Key to Japan's Competitive Success* (New York City, NY: McGraw-Hill, 1991), 126.

27 Daniel Markovitz, *Building the Fit Organization: Six Core Principles for Making Your Company Stronger, Faster, and More Competitive* (New York, NY: McGraw-Hill Education, 2016), 57.

28 Atul Gawande, *The Checklist Manifesto* (New York, NY: Picador), 48.

29 Masaaki Imai, *Kaizen (ky'zen): The Key to Japan's Competitive Success* (New York City, NY: McGraw-Hill, 1991), 23.

30 Robert Miller, *Hearing the Voice of the Shingo Principles: Creating Sustainable Cultures of Enterprise Excellence* (Abingdon, Oxfordshire: Routledge, 2018), 17.

31 Peter Hines and Chris Butterworth, *The Essence of Excellence: Creating a Culture of Continuous Improvement* (Caerphilly, UK: S A Partners, 2019), 17.

32 Ibid., 89.

33 Collin McLoughlin and Toshihiko Miura, *True Kaizen: Management's Role in Improving Work Climate and Culture* (Boca Raton, FL: CRC, 2018), xix.

34 Please note, this image follows an incomplete view of work as capacity instead of throughput, but the visual is valuable for understanding the different types of improvement.

35 Emily Adams and John Toussaint, *Management on the Mend: The Healthcare Executive Guide to System Transformation* (Appleton, WI: ThedaCare Center for Healthcare Value, 2015), 139.

36 Defined as a "creative crisis" where "most mass producers will need a crisis, what we have called a creative crisis, to truly change" by James Womack, Daniel Jones, and Daniel Roos, *The Machine that Changed the World* (Manhattan, NY: Simon & Schuster, 2007), 265.

37 "find that sense of urgency by clearly identifying and naming the crisis in order to convince staff that action is the only choice" from Emily Adams and John Toussaint, *Management on the Mend: The Healthcare Executive Guide to System Transformation* (Appleton, WI: ThedaCare Center for Healthcare Value, 2015), 139.

38 For a comical fun image that we need a burning platform to improve, see Kenneth Rolfes and William H. Baker Jr., *Lean for the Long Term: Sustainment is a Myth, Transformation is Reality* (Boca Raton, FL: CRC Press, 2015), 69.

39 Donald Dinero, *Training Within Industry: The Foundation of Lean* (New York, NY: Productivity Press, 2005), 11.

40 Shingeo Shingo, *A Study of the Toyota Production System* (Boca Raton, FL: Routledge, 1989), 80.

41 https://mediaproject.wesleyan.edu/103018/

42 It is a "dangerous oversimplification." Quoted in Peter Senge, *The Fifth Discipline* (Manhattan, NY: Random House Business, 2006), 144, 209.

43 Peter Senge, *The Fifth Discipline* (Manhattan, NY: Random House Business, 2006), 293.

44 Joseph E. Swartz and Mark Graban, *Healthcare Kaizen: Engaging Front-Line Staff in Sustainable Continuous Improvements* (Boca Raton, FL: CRC Press), 78–79.

45 Timothy R. Clark, *The 4 Stages of Psychological Safety: Defining the Path to Inclusion and Innovation* (Oakland, CA: Berrett-Koehler Publishers, Inc., 2020), 69–70.

46 Peter Senge, *The Fifth Discipline* (Manhattan, NY: Random House Business, 2006), 321.

47 Ibid.

48 Alfie Kohn, *Punished by Rewards: The Trouble with Gold Stars, Incentive Plans, A's, Praise, and Other Bribes* (Boston, MA: Mariner Books, 1993), 181.

49 Masaaki Imai, *Kaizen (ky'zen): The Key to Japan's Competitive Success* (New York City, NY: McGraw-Hill, 1991), 84.

Chapter 2

Lessons Learned from Lean Production

Most improvement offices or Lean consultants have attempted at least one of the following methods from the Lean Production System:

- Discontinuous Improvement Projects (A3s, PDCAs, Kaizen Events, etc.)
- Quality Control (QC) Circles
- Daily Management (Kata, Huddles, 5S, etc.)

Let me be clear – each method listed above is either a direct teaching of Lean or an adaptation of its principles. And it is true that each method can add value, but only in a system that sustains the outcomes. We must analyze each one to better understand which elements are intrinsic to Lean or situational add-ons that arose in a specific context. The latter should not be accepted as universally applicable, and we must be careful not to embrace every idea branded as "Lean" with open arms.

Our analysis for each method will be broken down into three parts:

1. An explanation of *the method*
2. *Lessons learned* from the Virtues of Empowerment at work
3. The Vices of Management responsible for its *shortcomings*

When added up, the lessons learned provide the context for Part II on Practice and lay the foundation for our model of the Lean Empowerment System. I sincerely hope our analysis of these common models will save you some time if you are in the early phases of your Lean journey.

DOI: 10.4324/9781032644134-4

Discontinuous Improvement Projects

The Method

The umbrella of discontinuous improvement covers many types of work. It makes a team slow down or step aside from a process to change it, the opposite of building a plane as you fly it. And it is what we traditionally think of as "improvement." This work includes, but is not limited to, A3s, PDCAs, Value Stream Analyses (VSA), Process Mapping, and Rapid Improvement Events (RIE). The project managers and process engineers on the central Improvement Team are the responsible few who are tasked with organizing and executing these projects. Their planning process mirrors traditional project management: a robust planning phase ends with the publication of a charter document that identifies a data-driven problem statement, an objective, deliverables, stakeholders, timeline, and cost. A formal sponsor accepts the terms of the charter before the project team is assembled. Then, the project manager chooses from a toolbox of catchy Lean Production tools to reach the agreed-upon objective. Some of the most popular tools are Root Cause Analysis (Ishikawa Diagram, Spaghetti Diagram, and 5 Why Analysis), Value Mapping, Statistical Control Charts, and Going to the Gemba (Ohno Circle and Leader Standard Work).

The Lessons Learned (Virtues)

No Virtues (Ordinary People, Peer Problem Solving, Kaizen, or Design)

None of the Virtues of Empowerment are visible in the deployment of discontinuous improvement projects. We will instead focus on four ancillary learnings in their absence.

Learning #1

Standard work is a common output of a discontinuous improvement project. Teams map their current state, identify areas of improvement, then execute changes toward a future state that is later codified in a new Standard. But, like a strategic document, standard work is simply a pretty piece of paper unless it is given a proper home within a system. It cannot be the final step of improvement. It must come sooner.

Learning #2

The execution and success of improvement projects in a decentralized organization is incredibly difficult to scale. There is no easy way to include frontline staff from dozens of offices, which dramatically reduces the likelihood of sustainment.

Learning #3

Local managers are not equipped to support staff in the work of improvement. A central improvement team still has merit, but their effectiveness is limited by our cultural dependence on discontinuous improvement and urgency.

Learning #4

The various tools associated with Discontinuous Improvement Projects are the best means of understanding processes (process mapping and value mapping), identifying root causes (5 Why, Fishbone Diagram, etc.) or documenting change (Standard Work). But their application requires prudence. There is a place for discontinuous improvement in Lean systems, but it should not be the primary response to waste or inefficiency.

The Shortcomings (Vices)

Project Dependence

Discontinuous improvement relies on the central management team and its project managers as the instrument of change.[1] The success of a project depends on the organizational skills, meeting cadence, and accountability of the project manager, which varies from leader to leader. A good project manager can foster interpersonal connection and remain attentive to the impact that change has on the human psyche. Yet, it is more common for managers to hire based on hard technical skills, engineering degrees or production experience, over soft skills. Project managers with both technical skills and interpersonal skills, those who can live in both worlds at once, are hard to find.

Also consider the lifecycle of change, assuming the project results in an improvement. An improvement may dissolve when the project manager leaves. The energy of an idea is often charged by the leader and loses its luster when the source is removed. The transfer of responsibility from the project manager to a local process owner is difficult in practice unless the process owner is intrinsically convinced by the merit of the change, or the frontline team was involved in the improvement process. There are countless handoffs in the process of discontinuous improvement where a legitimate improvement can fall by the wayside.

Urgency Dependence

Think about the process of preventing cancer in the human body. Healthcare has systematized the early identification of cancer through annual blood tests, scans, colonoscopies, or mammograms based on various risk factors. And many cancers, if caught early, can be treated. Yet, some patients choose to forgo the annual checks and instead monitor their body for changes. Those who wait for serious symptoms to appear run the risk of the cancer developing to an extent that requires extensive intervention because symptoms are less common in the early stages of cancer. And the higher the stage, the higher the urgency of response.

Inefficiency is also a cancer that plagues our work. It metastasizes from one process to another unless checked by a system. Leaders wait until they experience the symptoms of a problem and then channel extensive resources into fixing it. The little complaints and nuisances of frontline staff rarely draw enough attention until they grow into something more dangerous.

Discontinuous improvement projects are inherently based on urgency. They are done as reactions to symptoms. The idea for a project often comes from a departmental leader who identifies a problem based on instinct or data, and after getting the attention of some influential leader who deems the situation as critical enough to intervene. Systems that rely on discontinuous improvement projects are rarely designed to catch the variance or abnormality prior to disaster.

Finally, it is rare to find a unifying reason or goal that connects the various projects in motion. Each improvement project is treated as its own reaction to a problem and is separated from the organizational strategy (assuming one exists). According to Masaaki Imai, "the most glaring and significant shortcoming of Western management today is the lack of improvement philosophy."[2] Reacting to symptoms will give leaders the sense they have a deeper purpose when it is absent. Urgency gives the illusion of strategy. And urgent projects produce the illusion of progress.

QC Circles

The Method

Quality Control (QC) Circles are a popular tool for achieving local success by engaging the voice of the workforce. A QC Circle is a multidisciplinary team of frontline staff and management who meet on a regular basis (weekly, semi-weekly, or monthly) to identify problems and experiment with new processes. The team is facilitated by a manager or team leader who helps to focus attention, document experiments, and track results. The group is attractive for leaders due to its fairly simple design. But successful implementation requires preexisting standards and suggestion systems. Local experimentation is only sustainable if system-wide structures are already in place.

QC Circles have a high rate of failure in the West because visitors to Japanese factories will observe their success and seemingly simple design and launch them in a vacuum.[3] As a result, they fail to address the real systematic problems of its members.[4] Masaaki Imai argues that QC Circles are intended to be part (10–30%) of a program, not the program itself.[5] Leaders must remember that, in the words of Deming, QC Circles are the last step of an improvement system, not the first.[6,7]

The Lessons Learned (Virtues)

Ordinary People

Frontline staff remind administrators how ordinary people communicate. Corporate jargon isn't necessary. Endless acronyms are not a prerequisite for intelligence. And Lean isn't more successful when it is called "Lean." QC Circles tap into the basic human desire to try new things and see how they go. It doesn't rely on fancy Lean buzzwords to be successful. And, although a world without standards is, in the wisdom of Juran, a perpetual Tower of Babel,[8] one might also argue that our use of alienating language may lead to an unintentional Tower of Babel constructed on jargon and buzzwords.[9] Processes must be standardized. Descriptions of the system should not. Listen to what the people are saying, and how they are saying it.

Peer Problem Solving

A QC Circle is a safe environment to share ideas. It introduces peer problem solving at the local level. At its best, the representative of each role will consult her peers before implementing an idea and gather feedback after a launch. Peer problem solving allows staff to be nimble without relying on leadership to identify problems. It is change at its best.

Kaizen: Projects vs Experiments

Which term is better for describing improvements: Project or Experiment?

The word "project" implies a long-term and permanent change. It also expects perfection or at least success. Failure is unacceptable.

The word "experiment" implies a short-term and temporary change. Failure is an acceptable outcome. Staff are free to conduct "recreational experiments" that feel nice, help the flow of the practice, and give them a voice. In the words of Juran, "three cheers for success. Two cheers for efforts."[10] The number of ideas submitted will likely increase, and teams will feel energized by small wins around trivial problems before moving on to larger issues.[11]

Kaizen: Months vs Weeks

What is the best cadence for an experiment cycle?

The human brain conceptualizes weeks better than months. A month is less tangible and can start mid-week and end mid-week. Because of this, the number of workdays in a month can vary between twenty and twenty-three days. Although this seems small, the variable is four workdays: essentially a full work week. A month is perceived as a long time but is no longer than four weeks. For example, anyone will try a diet for two weeks, but a month seems like a serious commitment. We tend to overestimate how much we can reasonably accomplish in a single month, which makes the week a more reliable tool for estimating work.

Weeks are exact and tangible. They always have seven days and five workdays (excepting holidays). Projecting out an idea one week into the future is easy; if it is Tuesday today, we will reconvene next Tuesday. It is much harder to plan for a monthly recurrence without some level of confusion (i.e., the second Wednesday of each month will almost always land on a different numerical day). Staff are also more willing to trial a two-week experiment compared to a monthly project.

Design - Purposeful Siloes

The thought of creating siloes between teams is unpopular with most leaders. Leaders are afraid that our siloes encourage selfishness if we aren't fixing the value stream. We often hear the term, "steal from Peter to pay Paul." But the fear of "selfish Kaizens" or "isolated islands" is unfounded.[12]

Joseph E. Swartz and Mark Graban debunk the fear in their book, *Healthcare Kaizen*. So, consider the alternative: How can we intelligently discuss a value stream across multiple roles on a team when each one lacks their own standard? Consider the mathematical impact of a cross-functional change in this situation: a system becomes five times as chaotic if an experiment results in changes to five different roles that lack role-based standards. Role-based standards must be created before cross-functional standards.

Let us consider another unpopular opinion: an immature improvement system isn't capable of thinking longitudinally (across different jobs), only functionally.[13] Leaders of the Training Within Industry (TWI) program, the earliest incarnation of Standard Work, understood this exact idea. Two-thirds of the programs launched by TWI, Job Relations and Job Instructions, focused on a single employee or role, whereas Job Methods required "cooperation with others in the organization."[14] We must resist the urge to fix the value stream when there is waste in a single job code.

The Shortcomings (Vices)

Management Dependence

QC Circles often rely on management for facilitation. Departments with strong managers will have an unfair advantage over those with managers who are less enthusiastic or have lower levels of emotional intelligence. And the teams with disengaged or skeptical managers will almost immediately disband their QC Circles after the first roadblock. A manager poses an inherent risk to empowerment when she is the gatekeeper for the voice of staff.

Hero Dependence

Staff members are often handpicked for QC Circles based on their ability to identify problems and brainstorm solutions. The team relies on a few heroic individuals to generate strong ideas on their own. No matter how low the leaders set expectations, the members will self-impose a pressure to come up with massive ideas and, as a result, overlook the small things that bother them.

The frontline staff in the QC Circle are also too ordinary to enact sustainable changes. They have no true authority. And there is no reason (other than preexisting trust) for their peers to try their experiments. They must rely on the urgency of the problem at hand and aren't viewed as experts.

Urgency Dependence

It is common for leaders to apply pressures to scale the reach of QC Circles based on the success of a few teams. They want to push the "easy button" of empowerment without too much complexity. But they are not close enough to see the limitations. Without system-wide standards, department-specific processes will form. And, in the absence of design, the expansion of a local system only creates further chaos. Each improvement injects the team with the confidence that moves them further away from the possibility of future design. This becomes problematic if a system ever decides to pivot and launch an organization-wide standard. Claims of empowerment will be undermined and the relationship with frontline staff will be damaged.

At an extreme, the idea of scaling success is a flawed oversimplification and symbolic of incomplete design.[15] According to Westley, Zimmerman, and Patton, in their exploration of Complex Adaptive Systems (CAS):

> If the goal is social transformation, the next step is rarely obvious. It often means working on multiple fronts and paying attention to readying the system to respond to the innovation, as much as trying to duplicate the innovation…Scaling up is rarely a linear process that involves doing more of the same, like producing another cake by using the same recipe… Each success only increases the pressure to scale up, to find the tipping point where the innovation becomes the longed-for tidal wave of change.[16]

Daily Management

The Method

Daily Management takes many forms. There is value in having teams gather each day (preferably in the morning) to review the data from the previous day and identify opportunities to make today better. The use of simple tools – paper, markers, charts – is encouraged. One common form of daily management, a Daily Management Board, is based on Japanese Kamishibai, an ancient art of storytelling. A narrator, known as the kamishibaiya, used an emakimono, translated as "picture scroll," to tell a historical story. Staff are similarly encouraged to own the board and be hands-on, taking turns as the storyteller. The data tells a story.

The content of daily management can differ greatly between organizations. Some teams use a minimalist version of a Daily Management Board, simply assigning job duties and reviewing data. Others go further with the inclusion of experimentation sheets, Toyota Kata coaching, or other forms of improvement. Finally, we have seen Daily Management used as a tool for leaders to monitor and track the proficiency of staff in various job duties. Some formulas work better than others, and company culture remains the key driver of successful implementation.

The Lessons Learned (Virtues)

Design

I once heard a story from a leader who asked for feedback during a site visit: "What do you think about the most recent version of the Daily Management Board?" The registration staff, who had previously voiced her respect for the process, replied, "It's fine, and you know I won't sugarcoat things, so here it goes. The board essentially tells us to work harder and work faster… it really doesn't give us a way to get better."[17] This was a wakeup call for the leadership team. On its own, the daily review of data gave staff ownership and clarity, but it is not an improvement process. Access to data is only half of the battle.

The first part of system design for improvement is creating a workplace that "speaks back" to the employee.[18] Data and standards, the language of the workplace, are the basic universal needs of frontline staff. Each one uniquely equips those closest to the work with feedback about the current state of things. Then a system is responsible for orchestrating improvement. This step is organization-specific.

One of the most comprehensive and inclusive forms of improvement is Kata coaching. Kata is an iterative process, based on data, to move a team from their current state to a distant dream state by small improvements toward achievable goals.[19] Frontline staff identify a process they want to improve, map their future goal, current state, and next goal, and then brainstorm all the possible barriers that keep them from reaching that next goal. The team focuses on one barrier, then chooses a single experiment to overcome that barrier. The follow-up session, set on a recurring basis, follows the same script, and adds the question "What did you learn?"

Kata coaching is as useful for managers as the frontline staff. It is common for managers to attend a simple training workshop, receive a prescriptive coaching card, and then follow the flow of the board. A thirty-second to three-minute huddle each morning informs the manager about any major issue or exciting win for the entire team. Although they may express initial hesitation about the prescriptive process, they will quickly realize the Kata process and coaching card will both guide and limit the involvement of the manager. It signals to them: "Your voice really matters!"

The Shortcomings (Vices)

Urgency Dependence

Elton Mayo conducted a psychological study in 1924 that proved how the outcome of a test will improve when someone thinks they are being watched.[20] This phenomenon became known as the "Hawthorne Effect." But, as one could expect, the effects of being watched eventually wear off. Results will either return to their previous state or *get worse* because of the distrust sown by the close monitoring. The use of daily management will drive up scores, but at a cost. In addition, the motivation of staff is also at stake. People tend to lose interest in a task when they are carefully monitored.[21] Feelings of urgency will quickly wear off and staff must find within themselves a new motivation to continue improving. Leaders must quickly decipher the difference between a "flash-in-the-pan" or a sustainable change.

Daily management cannot be the single source of motivation because it is perceived as extra work. It is simply one piece of a system. In the words of Liker, "The board is not the cause of Continuous Improvement... When there is an effective process then the board becomes an aid to that process."[22]

Management Dependence - Control

Self-control is the goal of daily management. Control is generally defined as any act of introjection to influence the actions of another person or team toward some desired outcome. Self-control is markedly different, but still another form of control. It requires integration: making one's own value, understanding the rationale of the decision, and self-determination.[23] But, both control and self-control benefit the controller more than the controlled. They are management tools that assume a hierarchical structure and dependence on the need for management to hold the control instead of releasing it.

Teams who launch Daily Management Boards will often experience a common barrier: Staff *perception* differs from leadership *intent*.

Leaders, out of positive *intent*, buy in to the premise that Production Systems can only achieve statistical control through control or self-control. Everything they have been taught about efficiency is laced with control in the form of standard work, process audits, variation identification, and improvement. They have read about successful Lean leaders who find ways, using the carrot or the stick, to motivate people to do a better, more efficient process. These views are the norm.

But they fail to understand how the deployment of daily management in a Production System is *perceived* as management control hidden behind the façade of empowerment. And the only thing worse than authoritarianism is authoritarianism hiding behind the façade of democracy. The fear of false freedom is greater than the hope of true freedom.[24] As a result, staff become justifiably jaded by the remnants of past systems that made similar promises. They wait for the fabled day when the Daily Management Boards become elaborate wall décor.

The best option for leadership in this situation is to proactively address concerns before they are voiced. Perceptions must be quenched before they are enflamed. Here we can borrow from Alfie Kohn, renowned psychologist, who explains three steps to gain support for a topic that is not intrinsically interesting but necessary:

1. Acknowledge it may not seem interesting.
2. Explain long-term and short-term benefits.
3. Give staff as much control as possible.[25]

The disconnect between staff perception and leadership intent makes the implementation of daily management a risky business. An onlooker will have trouble deciphering the cultural success of daily management systems unless they interview staff and spend time with them. Improvements in data or daily adherence to a process are not measures of success: they are the most basic and preliminary requirements. The true measure of success is staff ownership; do staff continue to see value in daily management when their manager goes on vacation?

Management Dependence – Timetables

Training timetables are a common part of Daily Management used by managers in Lean Production Systems to achieve standardization in the absence of organization-wide standards.[26] A timetable is a visual chart posted by management that associates each job duty with a visual cue of proficiency for each staff. The visual cue may be a 4-square block, a pyramid, or a numerical count. The chart is meant to motivate staff to meet basic standards and reward peers who become experts in certain tasks. Management is responsible for updating the chart each week after conducting audits with the standard work document.

The timetable audit process is always the first element of daily management abandoned by managers, which inadvertently taints the entire system. Indifference toward an improvement system is contagious; teams started to neglect other parts of daily management when the manager's task is neglected, sometimes leading to total abandonment of the process. If staff associate other elements of daily management, truly value-added activities, with audits, which are perceived as non-value-added, the entire process is put at risk. And this is not a risk many systems can afford.

The cultural burden of audits outweighs the benefits to quality. Even the most respected and empathetic managers are uncomfortable auditing their teams. No amount of leader standard work or time in the Gemba can counterbalance the distrust sown in staff. They will question how managers are able to audit them in a process that they themselves are untrained to perform. What was once an attractive Lean tool of standardization, dialogue, and control is yet another control tactic. Cultural change won't be easy, but it shouldn't be painful.

Summary of Learnings

Let us now summarize the many lessons learned from this chapter into two categories: Learnings from Successes and Learnings from Shortcomings. We can glean the former from the Virtues of Empowerment and the latter from the Vices of Production that we saw in the stories and examples of this chapter. A formulaic categorization of both will lay the foundation for Part II, where a new model for Lean Empowerment will be proposed. The following is a list of needs or general learnings to consider.

Learnings from Successes (Virtues of Empowerment)

- **General**:
  - Discontinuous improvement projects embody none of the Virtues of Empowerment. But Lean tools (Process Mapping, Root Cause Analysis, etc.) can add value
  - Standard Work remains a pretty piece of paper until it is placed within a system
- **Ordinary People**:
  - Peers are more effective at supporting staff than local managers
  - Create a common language and reduce Lean jargon
- **Peer Problem Solving**:
  - Create a safe environment for peers to discuss ideas
  - Create a small group of change agents since not everyone wants to be part of improvement
  - Create purposeful siloes to understand roles before improving value streams across roles
- **Kaizen**:
  - Weeks are a better unit of measurement than months
  - Staff prefer the language of "experiments" over "projects"
- **Design**:
  - Allow recreational experiments
  - A workplace should "speak back" to the staff through data and standards
  - Access to data does not replace an improvement system
  - Be aware of the Hawthorne Effect (people improve when they know they are being watched)

Learnings from Shortcomings (Vices of Production)

- **Hero Dependence**:
  - Provide a formal coaching system for all managers regardless of coaching experience
  - Develop a "title" or system that gives ordinary people the authority to experiment
- **Management Dependence**:
  - Create a process of global improvement submission that doesn't rely on managers

- Create a support system from peers who know the job duties and standards

■ **Project Dependence**:
- Foster an increased comfort level for small improvements

■ **Urgency Dependence**:
- Clearly define the purpose for why we do improvement
- Deflect pressures to scale from leadership

The Virtues of Empowerment and the Vices of Production are the generous teachers of many lessons. Our ability to recognize them at work will increase once we have been introduced to their manifestations. The three common improvement tools reviewed in this section – Discontinuous Improvement Projects, QC Circles, and Daily Management – reveal many of their benefits and quirks.

The study of theory is helpful inasmuch as it improves practice. Part I set the context for Part II and laid the foundation for our model of the Lean Empowerment System. Our energy now shifts from the intangible to the tangible.

Notes

1 Emily Adams and John Toussaint, *Management on the Mend: The Healthcare Executive Guide to System Transformation* (Appleton, WI: ThedaCare Center for Healthcare Value, 2015), 72.

2 Masaaki Imai, *Kaizen (ky'zen): The Key to Japan's Competitive Success* (New York City, NY: McGraw-Hill, 1991), 29.

3 Ishikawa warns that "QC circle activities alone will not bring about Total Quality Control (TQC)" in Kaoru Ishikawa, *What is Total Quality Control? The Japanese Way* (1985), 94.

4 Masaaki Imai, *Kaizen (ky'zen): The Key to Japan's Competitive Success* (New York City, NY: McGraw-Hill, 1991), 19.

5 Ibid., 11, 47.

6 W. Edwards Deming, *Out of the Crisis* (Cambridge, MA: The MIT Press, 2018), 146.

7 For a comprehensive history of QC Circles, refer to Masaaki Imai, *Kaizen (ky'zen): The Key to Japan's Competitive Success* (New York City, NY: McGraw-Hill, 1991).

8 J. M. Juran, *Juran on Leadership for Quality: An Executive Handbook* (Florence, MA: Free Press, 1989), 106.

9 W. H. Baker and K. D. Rolfes, *Lean for the Long Term: Sustainment is a Myth, Transformation is Reality* (New York, NY: Productivity Press, 2017), 2.

10 J. M. Juran, *Managerial Breakthrough* (New York, NY: McGraw-Hill Book Co., 1995), 43.

11 Daniel Markovitz, *Building the Fit Organization: Six Core Principles for Making Your Company Stronger, Faster, and More Competitive* (New York: McGraw-Hill Education, 2016), 24.

12 Joseph E. Swartz and Mark Graban, *Healthcare Kaizen: Engaging Front-Line Staff in Sustainable Continuous Improvements* (Boca Raton, FL: CRC Press), 263. Shingeo Shingo, *A Study of the Toyota Production System* (Boca Raton, FL: Routledge, 1989), 155.

13 Emily Adams and John Toussaint, *Management on the Mend: The Healthcare Executive Guide to System Transformation* (Appleton, WI: ThedaCare Center for Healthcare Value, 2015), 37.

14 Donald Dinero, *Training Within Industry: The Foundation of Lean* (New York, NY: Productivity Press, 2005), 39.

15 Now this is not true for processes, which may require scaling beyond a pilot or series of experiments.

16 Frances Westley, Brenda Zimmerman, and Michael Patton, *Getting to Maybe: How the World is Changed* (Toronto, ON: Vintage Canada, 2007), 209, 207.

17 According to Training Within Industry – 16 – there is a difference between doing a job in less time and doing a job faster. The use of less time assumes true improvement, whereas working faster is likely the result of work at an unsustainable pace.

18 Collin McLoughlin and Toshihiko Miura, *True Kaizen: Management's Role in Improving Work Climate and Culture* (Boca Raton, FL: CRC, 2018), 46.

19 For more on Kata, read the 3 books by Mark Rother.

20 Peter Hines and Chris Butterworth, *The Essence of Excellence: Creating a Culture of Continuous Improvement* (Caerphilly, UK: S A Partners, 2019), 43.

21 Alfie Kohn, *Punished by Rewards: The Trouble with Gold Stars, Incentive Plans, A's, Praise, and Other Bribes* (Boston, MA: Mariner Books, 1993), 79.

22 Jeffrey K. Liker and George Trachilis, *Developing Lean Leaders at All Levels: A Practical Guide* (Jacksonville, FL: Lean Leadership Institute Publications, 2014), 174.

23 Alfie Kohn, *Punished by Rewards: The Trouble with Gold Stars, Incentive Plans, A's, Praise, and Other Bribes* (Boston, MA: Mariner Books, 1993), 251.

24 Also, "when people work in an environment day in and day out where they are used to being told what to do, are rarely asked what they think, are used to perceiving themselves as weaker... they develop a fear of freedom. Ingrained behavior doesn't just disappear." From Brenda Zimmerman, Curt Lindberg, and Paul Plsek, *Edgeware: Lessons from Complexity Science for Health Care Leaders* (Irving, Texas V H A Incorporated, 2008), 62.

25 Alfie Kohn, *Punished by Rewards: The Trouble with Gold Stars, Incentive Plans, A's, Praise, and Other Bribes* (Boston, MA: Mariner Books, 1993), 90.

26 Patrick Graupp and Martha Purrier, *Getting to Standard Work in Health Care: Using TWI to Create a Foundation for Quality Care.* (New York, NY: Productivity Press, 2022), 133.

PRACTICE

Chapter 3

The Lean Empowerment System

System, People, Process, and Technology

Some phrases stick with us like a tattoo on the brain. I recall a mantra from a book on IT leadership that outlined the order a leader must follow when proposing change: People, Process, and Technology. A little research uncovers the rich history of the idea:

> In 1964, Dr. Harold Leavitt, an American psychologist of management, developed a business management model called Leavitt's Diamond Model. This was made up of four aspects: people, tasks, structure and technology. Over time, Leavitt's Diamond was reimagined into *people, process* and *technology* (PPT), often as a Venn diagram or 'golden' triangle that combined tasks and structure into process.
>
> In the 1990s, a security technologist named Bruce Schneier championed PPT, turning it into a business practice "near-mantra." Sometimes referred to as a "three-legged stool," the people, process, technology model continues to be an important framework of effective organizational management to this day.[1]

This phrase is a universal ground rule for strategic decision-making and general improvement. It is a helpful reminder to first invest in the people, then review their processes, and finally apply a technological solution to fix

DOI: 10.4324/9781032644134-6

a problem. Many issues can be solved at the personal level without investing in expensive applications or tools.

We must augment the PPT model above with an important precondition to success: *a system*. We must look at all things through the lens of the "System, People, Process, and Technology." The chapters in this section are split into these four categories. They also leverage the combined learnings from successes and shortcomings (on pages 55–6). A cohesive picture emerges when we recategorize them under the new headings:

- **System**:
  - Clearly define the purpose for why we do improvement
  - Create a common language and reduce Lean jargon
- **People**:
  - Create a support system from peers who know the job duties and standards
  - Peers are more effective at supporting staff than local managers
  - Develop a "title" or system that gives ordinary people the authority to experiment
  - Create purposeful siloes to understand roles before improving value streams across roles
  - Create a small group of change agents since not everyone wants to be part of improvement
  - Create a safe environment for peers to discuss ideas
  - Provide a formal coaching system for all managers regardless of coaching experience
- **Process**:
  - Foster an increased comfort level for small improvements
  - Allow recreational experiments
  - Create a process of global improvement submission that doesn't rely on managers
  - Staff prefer the language of "experiments" over "projects"
  - Weeks are a better unit of measurement than months
  - Standard Work remains a pretty piece of paper unless it is placed within a system
  - Deflect pressures to scale from leadership
- **Technology**:
  - A workplace should "speak back" to the staff through data and standards
  - Be aware of the Hawthorne Effect (people improve when they know they are being watched)

- Access to data does not replace an improvement system
- Lean tools (Process Mapping, Root Cause Analysis, etc.) can add value, but are not enough

These guiding principles lead us to our definition of a Lean Empowerment System:

A self-organizing body of Lateral Leaders who improve Standard Work in a Kaizen Suggestion System

I strongly believe that an outline can be helpful for visualizing the progression of thought. Here is the linear flow of ideas through the following chapters that will expand on each part of the definition above:

- ■ **Chapter 4: System**: "A self-organizing body"
  - The Elements: Reductionism and Systems Thinking
  - The Relationship Between Elements: Trinitarian Theology
  - The Purpose of a System: Telos
  - Three System Models
    - Self-Organizing: Open-Source System
    - Self-Aware: Microsystem
    - Organic: Complex Adaptive System (CAS)
- ■ **Chapter 5: People**: "of Lateral Leaders"
  - Lateral Leaders
    - Change Agents
    - Attractors
    - Experienced Amateurs
    - The Gemba Incarnate
    - Artisans
    - Internal Consultants
    - Sensors
    - Induction Educators
  - The Job of Lateral Leaders
  - The Process Improvement Team
- ■ **Chapter 6: Process**: "who improve Standard Work in a Kaizen Suggestion System"
  - Kaizen
  - Suggestion System
    - The History: TWI (Training Within Industry)
    - The Context: Psychological Safety
    - The Data: Quantifying Improvement

Complexity Is Layered Simplicity

Let me remind the reader that our model is purposefully layered and home-grown. If it seems complex, it is because *it is* complex! A successful system is complex in theory but presented in a simple way that makes participants think, "Wow, this is easy. I could do that!" And it starts to come into focus when there are enough (but not too many) layers. Like an oil painting, a system becomes visible after seven or eight layers, given time to dry and cure. Each coat provides the foundation for the next coat and is composed of the same basic materials. But many layers of simplicity create a work of art with grand complexity.

Also keep in mind how the Toyota Production System is Toyota's work of art. It is the result of decades of problem solving and layering of ideas. It was born in a very specific context. And it continues to live in a very specific context. The Empowerment System outlined in this section is also the result of problem solving and learning in our contemporary context.

It directly serves knowledge workers in the 21st Century.[2] We hope this model is more applicable since it was born and lives in our current context.

Notes

1 https://www.procore.com/jobsite/the-foundation-of-successful-wfm-people-process-technology/

2 Michael Ballé and D. T. Jones, *The Lean Sensei: Go See Challenge* (Boston, MA: Lean Enterprise Institute, 2019), 73.

Chapter 4

System

Lean Empowerment System Definition:
A self-organizing body of Lateral Leaders who improve Standard Work in a Kaizen Suggestion System

> We can't control systems or figure them out. But we can dance with them![1]
>
> – Donella Meadows

Those who claim, "we have no system" are mistaken; there is always a system. But it might be unintentional. Organizations "MacGyver"[2] makeshift systems with administrative duct tape and cardboard committees until a more intentional system arrives. We default to "what works" until we find "what's right." Our systems, no matter how intentional or "MacGyvered," contain artifacts that can be studied.

The goal of this chapter is to help the reader understand systems theories and place the Lean Empowerment System in context. It is relatively short because systems theories are fairly contemporary and the literature is limited. Despite the infancy of the subject, we believe it is important to clarify some popular language in the study of systems since the rhetoric of Systems Thinking or "System-ness" has become popular among executive leadership as an off-the-cuff response to organizational opacity or a general lack of clarity. Although they have positive intent, the ideas voiced by these leaders are diluted or misguided versions of Systems Thinking as it is presented in academic literature.

DOI: 10.4324/9781032644134-7

The first step to understanding a new theory is learning the language. Systems have three universal components: elements, relationships (between elements), and a purpose.[3] We will start by discussing elements and how to understand common systematic problems. We will assess the two complementary yet different theories of Reductionism and Systems Thinking.

Then, we will illustrate the relationships between elements through a reflection on the theological mystery of the Trinity. Our lofty musings in this section may be obtuse to some readers, but the underlying idea is unparalleled in other disciplines.

Third, we will review the purpose of a system through the lens of the "Telos," a popular notion from Greek philosophy. And finally, we will shift our language from mechanical models to organic self-organizing bodies after an analysis of three popular system models: Open-Source Systems, Micro systems, and Complex Adaptive Systems (CAS).

The Elements: Reductionism and Systems Thinking

The term "system elements" can refer to people, teams, processes, language, or any other cultural construct. System theorists will debate on how to best understand these elements: do we reduce each system to bite-size pieces to be understood linearly (Reductionism), or do we take a broader view and observe the life cycles of elements (Systems Thinking)? Neither method is exhaustive, nor does it tell the full story of each element. This compels us toward a less combative and more collaborative view: Reductionism is complementary with Systems Thinking.[4]

Reductionism places each element under a microscope, which can both enhance the effectiveness of the whole system and limit it.[5] Focusing energy into one sub system can improve that area while at the same time overlooking the relationships between sub systems.[6] This is not dissimilar from the purposeful siloes introduced in Chapter 2 (Lessons Learned – QC Circles – Design). Staff must first understand the standards of their role before attempting to standardize or improve value streams across multiple roles. Injecting change into an unstable system will likely result in further chaos, making a strong case for Reductionism.

But Reductionism does not come naturally to the general public.[7] Let me explain with an illustration. Leidy Klotz, author of *Subtract*, conducted a study that was published in *Nature*.[8] He "investigated whether people are as likely to consider changes that *subtract* components from an object, idea or situation as they are to consider changes that *add* new components" (my emphasis added). His study placed a Lego structure before participants with the directions: "Improve this project so that it can hold a brick above the [figure's] head without collapsing." He found that participants were more likely to add blocks to balance the structure instead of subtracting, even though the experiment was purposefully designed to favor the latter as the best solution to the problem. In his words, "people systematically default to searching for additive transformations, and consequently overlook subtractive transformations." Klotz concluded that our cultural predisposition to solve problems through addition is problematic in situations that are better served by reduction. Adding more people, processes, or technology without first understanding the needs of a silo within a system can be counterproductive.

The theory of Reductionism fails to paint the full picture of system elements and requires balance from another model. Consider the two Greek words for time: chronos and kairos. Chronos represents the linear passing of time from one item to the next. Things happen when they happen. Alternatively, kairos is a cyclical or seasonal view of time. It is rooted in the belief that there is a *right* moment for something. In this context, we can now introduce the study of Systems Thinking. Systems Thinking follows the cyclical nature of kairos instead of the linear chronos of Reductionism. And it is echoed in Ecclesiastes 3:1: "for everything there is a season."

Chapter 2 hinted at the existence of systemic virtue and vice as a force beyond the virtue and vice of an individual person. Systems Thinking follows this thread and breaks down cycles into two similar categories: vicious cycles or virtuous cycles.[9] Virtuous cycles are "processes that reinforce in desired directions" and can elevate entire communities.[10] Virtue begets virtue. But vice also begets vice. Vicious cycles exacerbate existing problems and bring out the worst of human nature. As explained in the section on self-against and self-for in Urgency Dependence, a vicious cycle can aggravate patterns of fear and self-protection. They may even claim the lives of entire systems.

Each system will better understand its elements if it lets go and allows the natural oscillation between Reductionism and Systems Thinking, chronos and kairos, linear thinking and cyclical thinking. These two theories teach us how important it is to understand the individual building blocks of a system before understanding the interplay between elements. This takes us to the next phase in systems theory: relationship. Relationships are inevitable in a world of attraction and community.

The Relationship Between Elements: Trinitarian Theology

Contemplate the Trinity from Christian theology. It is comprised of three Persons: The Father, the Son, and the Holy Spirit. Each Person is distinct from the others, yet fully the others. This is one of the core mysteries of Christian theology and has been the topic of countless books throughout history. Theologians even argue that any image of the Trinity is blasphemous since we cannot fully comprehend its complexity. But the mystery is a perfect example of a system that has distinct elements and relationships between elements. The relationships between elements are the second part of a system.

It is common for the writings about Trinitarian theology to focus on the Persons (Figure 4.1) instead of the relationships between the Persons. We choose Reductionism when faced with mystery. Some theologians attribute the Old Testament to the Father, the New Testament to the Son, and the 2000 plus years of the Christian movement as the time of the Holy Spirit. But this view, albeit attractive, limits our understanding of the interplay between the three Persons of the Trinity. We owe this to the fact that "it's easier to learn about a system's elements then about its interconnections."[11]

Errors increase when we focus *only* on the elements and not the relationships. In healthcare, the caregivers and patients are the elements, but it is the relationship that matters. Take for example a referral between two physician offices. Both teams may be highly effective, but the sending of information (medical history, labs, imaging, etc.) and coordination of scheduling, or lack thereof, may result in missed or delayed care. Also consider the reaction of two medications in the human body. Both drugs may respectively heal an individual when taken on their own, but can have a damaging, or even lethal effect when mixed. The human body is a system of many elements in relationships. Understanding both the elements and their relationships is the best way to treat system disease, not just the symptoms.

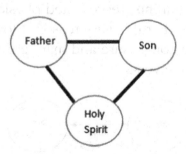

Figure 4.1 Traditional trinitiarian image.

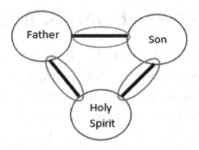

Figure 4.2 Relational trinitiarian image.

The relationship between each Person of the Trinity (Figure 4.2) is more complex and demands special attention. When studied, we can unveil unique qualities about each element while creating something entirely new. We learn more about each element when we view it through the lens of another. This expands our study of the Trinity into *six* studies: the Father, the Son, the Holy Spirit, the Father-Son relationship, the Son-Holy Spirit relationship, and the Father-Holy Spirit relationship. Each one helps unfold the mystery of the Trinity and increases the likelihood of a Christian to apply the concepts to her own life. And although the very studies of Christian theology and systems theories have a reputation of remaining somewhat abstract, the ultimate purpose is to help increase understanding and grow our faith. At the center of theological understanding is deepened relationship with God. And at the center of systems theory is improved relationship with those in the system.

Some theologians take this idea further and claim the Holy Spirit *is the relationship* between the Father and the Son, expressed as love (Figure 4.3). This interpretation of the relational nature of the Trinity invites us to consider the possibility of *relationships as elements* themselves. The closest that humans will get to this experience is the conception of children, the ultimate co-creative act. The child is both an element and embodiment of the relationship between the parents, represented physically in attributes, and spiritually through nurture. For this very reason, I love meeting the parents of my closest friends. The composure and mannerisms of the parents tell a lot about the child, and vice versa.

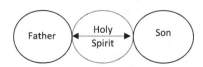

Figure 4.3 Holy Spirit as relationship in trinitarian image.

No matter the theological stance taken by the reader, we can learn the importance of the relationships between elements by dwelling on the mystery of the Trinity.

The Purpose of a System: Telos

Systems Thinking is "the ability to understand these interconnections [relationships between elements] in such a way to achieve a *desired* purpose."[12] Greek philosophy defines this purpose or goal as a *telos*. The telos of each human life is *eudaimonia*, translated as fulfillment, which is imprinted on our very nature. We are drawn toward fulfilling experiences and repelled by ones that are emptying. Something within us can identify each one without being told what to look for.

Systems help us see the gap between our current state and our goal (telos). We discern between what we want, the "espoused purpose," and what we are actually producing, our "current purpose."[13] Peter Senge uses the image of a rubber band held between two hands to visualize this state of mind. Imagine one hand, which represents vision, pulling the band upward as another hand, which represents current reality, pulls the band down. Each system holds a "creative tension" between its current reality and vision.[14] In the words of Womack, this "creative tension involved in solving complex problems in precisely what has separated manual factory work from professional 'think' work in the age of mass production."[15] A system can either lower its standards (vision) or move its current reality closer to that vision through action. The experience is felt by some as stress or tension, whereas others feel the same tension as a deep sense of longing or magnetic pull toward fulfillment.

The goal of fulfillment and the creative tension in a system assume that we live in a state of incompletion, and we spend our lives seeking completion. Christian theology explains this mystery in Genesis 1:27: we are made in the Image of God, pursuing the Likeness of God. Jesus was the only person who was fully Image and fully Likeness. The rest of us are made in the Image but strive through our actions to share in the Likeness. St. Augustine expands on this idea in the famous quote: "I am restless, Oh Lord, until I rest in you." And, as many saints and mystics throughout the course of history have learned, our path to eudaimonia is built with virtue, while vice distances us from fulfillment. The same logic follows for a system; virtuous cycles expand and vicious cycles contract.

Recall from Chapter 1 that virtue must be understood in communal terms. Actions either build up or tear down a community. Nothing happens in a vacuum, removed from relationship. We are fully dependent on relationships with others to reach our telos of fulfillment. And each element in a system finds its purpose in the relationship between elements, not the element itself.

The three components of a system – the elements, relationships, and functions (teloi) – are visible in both intentional and "MacGyvered" systems. You will start to see each one at play as you walk around your office or reflect on your last family reunion. They are inescapable; ingrained in our human existence and woven through the very thread of our being.

Let us now observe how these various ideas are embodied in three common system models: Open-Source Systems, Microsystems, and Complex Adaptive Systems (CAS). Each model will respectively increase our growing appreciation and understanding of systems theory as self-organizing, self-aware, and organic.

Three System Models

Self-Organizing: Open-Source System

We introduced a complex idea in the previous chapter that demands unpacking: A system may become *both* an independent system of relationships between elements *and* an element in a larger system. According to Meadows, this is how a system can cause its own behavior.[16] It gains the unique ability to *self-organize* since it contains the elements and relationships necessary to progress toward a telos. This behavior mimics the Holy Spirit, which is at the same time an element and a relationship. It also appears in pedagogy, the field of educational philosophy. We have all heard the phrase "The knowledge is already in the room and must simply be drawn out." This is better known as Constructivism, which argues how students do better at learning new information if they construct meaning through their experiences and attach it to the new content. They are not empty vessels waiting to be filled. Quite the opposite. Attempts to fill students with outside ideas may even be counterproductive since the system already has the necessary resources to reach its telos. Sometimes we just need to think inside the box.

A self-organizing system also threatens power structures and promotes unpredictability.[17] Charismatic movements in religion, inspired by the gifts of the Holy Spirit (1 Cor 12), or drawing on the vast expanse of "spirituality," are perceived as threats to conventional Christianity. Constructivism is a threat to passive forms of education such as lecturing or memorization. And, most pertinent to this book, self-organizing systems like the Lean Empowerment System threaten traditional Lean Production Systems. It pulls the rug of predictability out from underneath organizations, de-emphasizing tools of certainty (control charts, standard work, and data) and instead taps into human potential. The tools are not cast aside but reframed in the context of relationship.

The online encyclopedia, Wikipedia, and the open-source operating system, Linux, are two organizations that depend on self-organization for success. In his book *Drive*, Daniel Pink coins the term "open-source organization" in reference to a system where anyone can access the source code, has a voice to submit changes, and is at the same time held accountable by peers.[18] Open-source is a chaotic model since anyone can contribute. But it also stirs up unbounded innovation and peer engagement. It relies on self-policing and continual improvement to avoid stagnancy. And it gives staff an atmosphere that is decidedly not fail-safe, but where they are safe-to-fail.

Self-Aware: Microsystem

The following review of microsystems relies heavily on a nine-part series of articles published in the early 2000s by The Joint Commission in the Journal of Quality Improvement. The purpose of the series is clearly stated:

> [This] series of articles on microsystems is intended to provide useful ideas and methods that can be used in diverse clinical settings—outpatient, inpatient, skilled care, and home care—to create the conditions for sustained improvement in clinical quality and value in a way that is appreciated by patients and exciting to the front-line staff who serve them.

A clinical microsystem is generally defined as a small team of people who work together on a regular basis to provide care.[19] For this section we will expand this definition beyond clinical microsystems and consider *non-clinical microsystems.* The development of these macrosystems and microsystems is split into six phases:

1. A self-aware microsystem (m1)
2. A group of like microsystems (m1 + m1 + m1)
3. A group of unlike microsystems (m1 + m2 + m3)
4. A group of microsystems in relationship with a macrosystem (m1 + m2 + m3...+M1)
5. A group of like macrosystems (M1 + M1 + M1...)
6. A group of unlike macrosystems (M1 + M2 + M3...)[20]

The growth of a self-aware microsystem (m1) requires purposeful siloes. Each role must define its own success criteria and standards. Then, like microsystems (m1+m1+m1) develop a "common vocabulary for change as well as a common understanding of the barriers and constraints in process improvement. It [is] then possible to share and replicate best practices and change concepts among these like microsystems."[21] The foundation of peers helping peers is formed in Phase 2. Staff who share the same job code in multiple locations can also share best practices and learnings with each other.

Phase 3 is the collaboration between unlike self-aware microsystems (m1 + m2 + m3) to serve independent goals (teloi). The introduction of unlike microsystems can be messy and create healthy tensions as purposeful siloes are replaced with value streams. This is a steppingstone to the unified telos in Phase 4.

In Phase 4, a group of unlike microsystems forms around the goal (telos) of a macrosystem (m1 + m2 + m3...+ M1). This process naturally occurs as "systems evolve over time and are often embedded in larger systems/organizations."[22] At this point, the microsystems have gained the "self-understanding, ability to change, and ability to track and reflect on its performance," which allows it to "engage its context—the macrosystem in which it works and other microsystems with which it regularly interacts."[23]

A megasystem forms in Phase 5 and 6 between major departments (like or unlike) within an organization. Each macrosystem requires a strategic direction and solid structure before this phase is possible. Consider the partnership between an Information Technology (IT) department, Operations team, and Human Resources. The complexity grows as more layers are added that have layers of their own.

Microsystems are transactional by nature, but the currency isn't trade. It is collaboration. Koznik poetically introduces the metaphor of "Fair Trade" to understand the interactions within and between microsystems:

> The willingness and openness to support reciprocal action within a macrosystem is similar to the concepts of fair trade within a social economy…The fair-trade metaphor supports the idea that members need to trade with one another. If a member does not participate, the system will deny that member the benefits of trading—or in this case, collaborating. Those nonparticipating microsystems are then forced to seek support or relief from "stress" from other nonparticipating microsystems. Ultimately the value of participation will drive all microsystems to participate simply to survive as well as to be a part of the community with its associated family relationship.[24]

Microsystems are a systematic and tiered theory for understanding elements, relationships, and the functions of systems. It is quite different from the seemingly chaotic self-organization of open-source systems. And although the phased approach can equip organizations with the macro and mega systems toward which they may aspire, Meadows reminds us how "relationships *within* each subsystem are denser and stronger than relationships *between* subsystems."[25] This very point is a constant across all system models. The relationships between elements in the most basic subsystem, a microsystem (Phase 1), are the core building blocks of more complex systems. Complexity is layered simplicity. And we return once again to the importance of subsidiarity, or the assignment of power to the smallest or most local level. Each phase is not only a progression from the prior phase, but an extension.

Organic: Complex Adaptive System (CAS)

Leaders frequently use the language of a "well-oiled machine" to describe a work unit that functions seamlessly. Nobody bats an eye at this and other mechanistic phrases to describe human behavior because they are commonplace and meant as compliments.[26] The theory of Complex Adaptive Systems (CAS) challenges this and other misuses of mechanical adjectives to describe human behavior in the workplace and favors organic imagery in their place. In the words of Zimmerman, Lindberg, and Plsek, authors of

Edgeware and CAS theorists, "the metaphor of systems as mechanical or machine has shaped our studies in physics, biology, economics, medicine and organizations. Complexity is about reframing our understanding of many systems by using a metaphor associated with life and living systems rather than machines or mechanical systems."[27] Organizations are organic communities, not machines.[28] Our language must catch up.

It makes sense that our society prefers mechanistic language while at the same time depending heavily on Production Systems as models for work. The two are remnants of early 20th century industrial growth. But a shift from Production Systems to an Empowerment System will also herald in a shift from mechanistic images of human work to more organic images.

One popular organic image already exists in the apostle Paul's letter to the Christian community in Corinth. He uses the image of a human body to represent a community in one of the most quoted passages from Scripture:

> Indeed, the body does not consist of one member but of many. If the foot would say, "Because I am not a hand, I do not belong to the body," that would not make it any less a part of the body. And if the ear would say, "Because I am not an eye, I do not belong to the body," that would not make it any less a part of the body. If the whole body were an eye, where would the hearing be? If the whole body were hearing, where would the sense of smell be? But as it is, God arranged the members in the body, each one of them, as he chose. If all were a single member, where would the body be? As it is, there are many members yet one body.
>
> *(1 Cor 14–20)*

Organic language is also common in healthcare. Medical professionals are taught to view the body as a complex system of systems, not simply a machine to be tuned up and fixed. Each patient that walks through the door is a microcosm of lifestyle choices, family histories, environmental influences, and other social determinants of health. They are as complex, if not more, as the very system trying to provide care. A care team trapped in their mechanical worldview is ill equipped to confront such an intricate system of interconnections and poses a risk to the patient. So, like Osteopathic medicine, a field focused on caring for the whole person, our focus must change from response to prevention. Both caregivers on the frontlines and healthcare administrators must accept the challenge to make the switch to organic language. And any other organization can follow suit.

Lean Production Systems only scratch the surface of Systems Thinking. They suffer from a single-minded focus on individual elements and the value streams between elements (relationships) yet fail to recognize the relationships between human beings in the value streams. Its teloi include profits and productivity, with the elements and interconnections consigned as means to the end.

The Lean Empowerment System bets on the untapped human potential in a system. System elements and relationships are both means and ends in themselves, self-organizing, self-aware, and organic. Like the Holy Spirit, an entirely new and distinct element can form out of the interconnection between two other elements. We must continue our journey from systems to people, the face of a system.

Notes

1 Donella H. Meadows, *Thinking in Systems* (Chelsea, VT: Chelsea Green Publishing, 2008), 170.
2 MacGyver is a popular movie character from the mid-1980s who is known for his quick thinking and unconventional methods of using the regular items around him to get out of dangerous situations. A former co-worker of mine used this term to illustrate how our default systems are distinct from intentional systems.
3 Donella H. Meadows, *Thinking in Systems* (Chelsea, VT: Chelsea Green Publishing, 2008).
4 Ibid., 6.
5 David Peter Stroh, *Systems Thinking for Social Change: A Practical Guide to Solving Complex Problems, Avoiding Unintended Consequences, and Achieving Lasting Results* (Chelsea, VT: Chelsea Green Publishing, 2015), 31.
6 Donella H. Meadows, *Thinking in Systems* (Chelsea, VT: Chelsea Green Publishing, 2008), 83.
7 Leidy Klotz, *Subtract: The Untapped Science of Less* (New York, NY: Flatiron Books, 2022).
8 https://www.nature.com/articles/s41586-021-03380-y
9 According to Stroh, "Reinforcing feedback is the basis for what we know as virtuous and vicious cycles" in David Peter Stroh, *Systems Thinking for Social Change: A Practical Guide to Solving Complex Problems, Avoiding Unintended Consequences, and Achieving Lasting Results* (Chelsea, VT: Chelsea Green Publishing, 2015), 46.
10 Peter Senge, *The Fifth Discipline* (Manhattan, NY: Random House Business, 2006), 81.

11 Donella H. Meadows, *Thinking in Systems* (Chelsea, VT: Chelsea Green Publishing, 2008), 14.

12 David Peter Stroh, *Systems Thinking For Social Change: A Practical Guide to Solving Complex Problems, Avoiding Unintended Consequences, and Achieving Lasting Results* (Chelsea, VT: Chelsea Green Publishing, 2015), 16.

13 Ibid., 17.

14 Peter Senge, *The Fifth Discipline* (Manhattan, NY: Random House Business, 2006).

15 James Womack, Daniel Jones, and Daniel Roos, *The Machine That Changed the World* (Manhattan, NY: Simon & Schuster, 2007), 102.

16 Donella H. Meadows, *Thinking in Systems* (Chelsea, VT: Chelsea Green Publishing, 2008), 34.

17 Ibid., 79.

18 Daniel Pink, *Drive: The Surprising Truth About What Motivates Us* (New York, NY: Riverhead Books, 2011), 30.

19 Paul B. Batalden, et al., Microsystems in Health Care: Part 5. How Leaders Are Leading. *Joint Commission Journal on Quality and Safety*, 296 (2003): 298. doi:10.1016/s1549-3741(03)29034-1

20 Linda K. Kosnik and James A. Espinosa, Microsystems in Health Care: Part 7. The Microsystem as a Platform for Merging Strategic Planning and Operations. *Joint Commission Journal on Quality and Safety*, 29.9 (2003): 453. doi:10.1016/s1549-3741(03)29054-7

21 Ibid.

22 Ibid.

23 Paul B. Batalden, et al. Microsystems in Health Care: Part 9. Developing Small Clinical Units to Attain Peak Performance. *Joint Commission Journal on Quality and Safety*, 29.11 (2003): 582. doi:10.1016/s1549-3741(03)29068-7

24 Linda K. Kosnik and James A. Espinosa, Microsystems in Health Care: Part 7. The Microsystem as a Platform for Merging Strategic Planning and Operations. *Joint Commission Journal on Quality and Safety*, 29.9 (2003): 459. doi:10.1016/s1549-3741(03)29054-7

25 Donella H. Meadows, *Thinking in Systems* (Chelsea, VT: Chelsea Green Publishing, 2008), 83.

26 This is similar to the rampant use of military or sports metaphors that encourage competition over community.

27 Brenda Zimmerman, Curt Lindberg, and Paul Plsek, *Edgeware: Lessons from Complexity Science for Health Care Leaders* (Irving, Texas V H A, Incorporated, 2008), 18.

28 Peter Senge, *The Fifth Discipline* (Manhattan, NY: Random House Business, 2006), 269.

Chapter 5

People

Empowerment System Definition:
A self-organizing body *of Lateral Leaders* who improve Standard Work
in a Kaizen Suggestion System

Lateral Leaders

Consider the direction that opinions and complaints flow: laterally between
peers. Rumors and gossip travel faster and have more influence than any
corporate memo or workflow bulletin.[1] Simply observe the flurry of messages in a group-text between nurses! This momentum also exists in the
family unit, where communication is the strongest between siblings, or in
schools, where student consensus rules the day. Knowledge is like a pinball
machine, launching ideas into play, bouncing off walls, bumping into barriers, and eventually becoming lost to the trough, making room for a new
idea. The winning score compounds as more and more ideas travel the
lifecycle of thought to reality.

Organizations must learn how to follow this somewhat jumbled and
chaotic flow of ideas *laterally* instead of relying on *linear* structures. Linear
systems are more limited than lateral systems since they are built on a
foundation of waste, namely, the waste of movement. Lean Production
Systems traditionally define movement as the actions of people from one
station to another. But, in the Lean Empowerment System, the movement of

communication away from the source of an issue is a more dire type of waste. Lean leaders must shift their focus on the movement of *ideas* instead of *people*.[2]

Even at its best, a linear system will cap out way below the potential impact of a lateral system. We see this in the daily management of tiered huddles to improve communication flow, or the deployment of suggestion boxes to elicit feedback from staff. Although each has value, they lock ideas in a lateral flow from the frontline to management, or management to the frontline. They hinge on the false assumption that ideas cannot be solved where they arise. Leaders must acknowledge this assumption to take the first step toward freeing ideas from the waste of movement. As a result, they will no longer need to come up with creative ways to elicit ideas from staff or launch another newsletter to share information. They must simply let peers solve the problems of peers.[3]

Including peers in the generation and transmission of ideas means choosing lateral thinking instead of linear thinking. The Lean Empowerment System relies on lateral thinking whereas linear thinking is associated with the core sciences and traditional Lean or Six Sigma. But linear thinking is our default mode; it is logical, and outcome driven. At an early age, students are trained in the scientific method, the epitome of linear thought, because it is objective and reliable. This carries with them into the business world. Linear thinking is also concerned with finding a *solution* whereas lateral thinking is about *learning from the process*. The phrase "jumping to conclusions" reflects this sentiment. On the other hand, lateral thinkers explore the root cause of a problem or brainstorm creative alternatives. They are interested in learning from the process. Consider two math teachers who embody linear and lateral thinking. The math teacher who grades on the correctness of the final answer and nothing else represents linear thought. It is either fully right or wrong. Lateral thinking is embodied in the math teacher who gives partial credit based on the correctness of the work shown, in addition to the final answer. She cares equally about the process and the solution.

Lateral thinkers employ a multidisciplinary approach for understanding a topic to enhance their learning process. We see this in the healthcare arena. Countless articles have been published in healthcare journals over the past few decades that reiterate the importance of multidisciplinary teams of caregivers. The best clinicians from different fields are brought together to enhance quality of care, especially in complex fields like cancer diagnosis and treatment. The purpose is to come to a solution without isolating a single problem and addressing it with a single medicine, therapy, or treatment. Instead, both the care team and the patient are educated in the process as they collaborate to provide holistic care for the patient and address the overlap between multiple comorbidities. Healthcare organizations refer to these lateral care teams as "institutes."

Outside of an institute or team, each one of us must foster a multidisciplinary mindset and not focus all our learning into one academic pursuit. For example, the earliest philosophers were great because they were not just philosophers. Aristotle was an astronomer, biologist, geographer, and literary critic. Isaac Newton was a mathematician, physicist, historian, and chemist. These renowned thinkers understood that innovation in a field of study rarely comes from within the same field. It requires stepping outside into a neighboring view. In the words of a platitude from systems thinking, "you cannot dig a new hole by digging the same hole deeper."

The Lean Empowerment System is founded on lateral thinking. And it is embodied in an archetype we will refer to as a Lateral Leader. The entire Lean Empowerment System revolves around the Lateral Leader, like the solar system around the sun. This is not a top-down or bottom-up model: it is **peer-to-peer**. Because, at its best, top-down management results in clear direction, solid results, and data-driven implementation. And at its worst, staff are distrustful of leadership and strategy is lost in translation. Recent literature challenges the top-down model and promotes a bottom-up philosophy with ideas and changes coming from the frontline. This can promote high staff engagement and the quick identification of problems. But without a cogent system, a wholly bottom-up model of empowerment with free rein can lead to chaos. In the words of Senge, "To empower people in an unaligned organization can be counterproductive."[4] It is ultimately unsustainable. That is why the Lateral Leader is our best hope to lead a sustainable culture change in any industry where there are multiple staff sharing the same job title, either collocated or decentralized. This model of peer support has existed in many professional fields but is limited to *train the trainers* in education or *subject matter experts* in instructional design. And even worse, these peer-to-peer models are mainly used as vehicles for the dissemination of top-down agendas. They borrow elements of bottom-up management but repackage control in the giftwrap of empowerment. But true peer-to-peer management demands its own model: the Lateral Leader in the Lean Empowerment System.

The Lateral Leader has gone by many names throughout the works of American (Deming, Juran, Shewhart, Toussaint) and Japanese (Shingo,

Ohno, and Imai) engineers. Before we discuss their day-to-day work, let us explore the many faces of the Lateral Leader through the different names they have been called:

- Change Agents
- Attractors
- Experienced Amateurs
- The Gemba Incarnate
- Artisans
- Internal Consultants
- Sensors
- Induction Educators

Change Agents

Primary Source: *Toussaint*

Dr. John Toussaint, former CEO of ThedaCare in Wisconsin, said that we must look for "*change agents*" when we start an improvement journey.[5] How do we recognize these agents of change? They have always been around, but they are right where you don't expect them. "They will be complainers and local agitators who hear about lean and seize upon it to make the changes they want."[6] These complainers and detractors, who are fed up and vocal about inefficiencies, are sleeper cells within an organization; leaders must simply "unleash their capabilities."[7] The maverick who was once the most challenging liability in a traditional management system becomes the most valued asset in an empowerment system.[8] And, like a child whose lifelong identity was formed around titles like "naughty kid," or being "bad at school," employees who have always been described as "difficult" or a "complainer" may not think they have the "capacity to lead major change."[9] It is the responsibility of the organization to invest in these individuals and assume risk on behalf of their actions.[10]

Creating change agents out of detractors will require the support of leadership. Timothy Clark, leading thinker in psychological safety, states this eloquently: staff must have "cover in exchange for candor."[11] A great example of candor exists at Pixar Animation Studios. Pixar created and first coined the "Braintrust," which is a team of employees who watch a movie early in the animation process to provide direct feedback and comments.[12] The members of the Braintrust are given cover by leadership in exchange for their candor. Their valuable complaints and ideas help guide the animators and directors toward a timeless film. In a similar way, each leader must also give its change agents, the Lateral Leaders, cover in exchange for candor.

The theory of Complex Adaptive Systems (CAS) defends detractors. It argues that troublemakers are simply misunderstood. For example, management may not see their ideas as innovative, but "in cultures that are adaptive and change… troublemakers are the movers who push organizations to their creative edges, where new opportunities emerge."[13] I have found that detractors and complainers are the easiest to pick out in crowd of peers since their voice is the loudest and most impressionable on both peers and leaders. In many cases, their peers have already designated them as an informal figurehead. The organization needs only to catch up.

Attractors

Primary Sources: *TWI (Training Within Industry), Shingo*

The very foundation of systems theory rests on attraction; the relationship between two forces is equally important as the forces themselves. Consider the Earth revolving on an axis between its magnetic poles. The two poles are desolate and uninhabitable, but the force of their relationship allows for the presence of life in-between. Or recall the image of the Trinity and the relationships between each Person. Attraction is the source of Relationship.

There are *attractors* in every human community.[14] Consider the life of a party, the matriarchal powerhouse who insists on coming together, or the dinner guest that knits a quilt of conversation between strangers. These attractors "hold a system in its current pattern or propel it to a new pattern. They are the stable factors within system dynamics. And they represent the general trend of a system around which the details congregate."[15] Lateral Leaders are Attractors within an Empowerment System.

Attraction is the result of shared opinions. We are drawn to others by their presentation of ideas in the form of jokes, affirmations, or challenges. In a similar fashion, Lateral Leaders are aware that opinions are the currency of the frontline and data is the currency of management. And conversion from one to the other requires observation, keeping the pulse on both the impact of change (fact) and the perceived impact of change (opinion). Attractors watch these patterns shift and know when to provoke new patterns of interactions. They do this by introducing new elements into the conversation to help the entire system move toward its goal (telos).[16] We see the attractor in action across the history of Lean thinking, especially in the early Training Within Industry guides on standard work that encouraged leaders to "get the facts," but to not limit facts to objective data.[17] The Lateral Leader does not have enough operational power to create a new standard or strategy on her own, but she can inject new opinions and voices into a conversation.

Shingeo Shingo explains how the Toyota Production System defines to staff the know-how (standard) and know-why (strategy) of a job, but rarely defines the know-who (connection) and know-when (timing).[18] Leadership is responsible for setting strategy and standards, whereas staff are best attuned to the social dynamics of a team. These include connection and timing. A person's awareness of this dynamic determines the potential influence she may achieve in an organization. Because the most influential member on a team is the person to whom others stop and listen, and those who are the sounding board for complaints. For this reason, nominating the first round of Lateral Leaders is often an easy process since there are already staff among the ranks who are the "go-to" people for questions. By means of attraction, these peers elicit the questions, opinions, and complaints of their peers. And by virtue of their shared job title, the Lateral Leader will always have more influence among their peers than an administrator will ever dream to achieve.

Experienced Amateurs

Primary Sources: *Juran, Deming, Shewart*

Juran first coined "experienced amateurs" during his observations of quality among staff. These important team members are experts in their respective area of work, but amateurs in formal quality activities such as Total Quality Management (TQM), Lean, Six Sigma, etc. Juran argued how these experienced amateurs "should themselves become proficient in using the methods and tools of modern quality planning. This emergence consensus requires a massive cultural change."[19] In his eyes, the cultural challenge at hand is to train front-line staff to become fluent in process improvement. Although this may seem self-evident for a sustainable change in culture, many improvement methodologies drawing on Juran's influence rarely call on the expertise of the experienced amateur. Popular Six Sigma programs start by training executive leaders who will eventually cascade quality methods to their teams. The frontline is often three or four levels removed, and programs may fizzle or lose support before the experienced amateurs receive the most basic level of training. Or process engineers include frontline staff in value-mapping sessions to speak for their entire role with little preparation or follow-up. Any conversation with staff at the frontlines will indicate the same problem: Those with the most knowledge about a process are often the last consulted.

Deming's forward to Walter Shewhart's seminal work *Statistical Method from the Viewpoint of Quality Control* expands on this sentiment.[20] He explains that a standard, which is first created by a subject matter expert, may at any time be challenged and replaced by a new standard by other experts if their method produces superior outcomes. These process changes do not damage the pride of the expert who wrote the standard because highly skilled people in a particular task show less bias.[21] In what amounts to be an otherwise objective and statistically driven text, Deming appeals to the need for a gatekeeper who understands data and standards but is trusted enough as an expert in the standard to challenge its most basic assumptions. The person who was once defined as an amateur must be recognized as an expert in the subject matter. Our experienced amateur rises to the rank of the Lateral Leader. She "holds the responsibility for the use of the data."[22]

The Gemba Incarnate

Primary Source: *Imai*

The Gemba is one of the most discussed topics in recent Lean literature. Managers are encouraged to "go to the Gemba," or the place where work is done to hear the voice of frontline staff.

There are two different methods for going to the Gemba that have their own merits:

1. Management by walking around (MBWA) – random unplanned visits to frontline staff[23]
2. Gemba Walks – scheduled visits by leaders who follow leader standard work and ask frontline staff specific questions[24]

Most leaders will admit that they do not spend enough time at the frontline. In response, Gemba Walks were designed to prod managers out of their offices and into the workplace. At face value, it is hard to argue that listening to staff in their workplace is detrimental. But going to the Gemba without a game plan or systematic method of improvement can have the opposite effect as intended. The visit can be perceived by frontline staff as an attempt by management to stay relevant, or a mandatory task the manager must "check off" for the sake of optics. The simple act of showing up to ask a few questions makes little sustainable impact without a system that can understand and execute the ideas generated.

Gemba walks generate more waste in the name of empowerment.[25] For example, a scheduler may complain to a C-Suite leader about a workflow in their registration software. The C-Suite leader, out of an innate desire to fix the problem, escalates the concern to the respective team who is responsible for the improvement. Here we risk circumventing standard processes since the idea, now backed by the job title of the leader, receives more attention than other ideas from staff. It distracts the C-Suite leader from the work of strategy, overlooks the power of Lateral Leaders who are closer to the issue, and circumvents regular processes for ideas or improvements.

But the COVID-19 pandemic in 2020 broke the loop and forced administrators to rethink the value of Gemba walks. Visits to the Gemba decreased due to the risk of viral transmission. And the voice of staff was at risk of going unheard as administration moved to remote work. Some managers watched as issues unfolded and the great resignation peaked on the horizon. Others brainstormed innovative ways to engage staff remotely. Gone were the days of developing leader standard work questionnaires or executive rounding schedules. In their place, some organizations started to look forward to technology rather than looking back at the foundations of Lean thinking. Let us explore both to set the stage for the Lateral Leader.

Looking Back: Masaaki Imai, disciple of Taiichi Ohno at Toyota Motors, devised the concept of the "Kaizen man." This was a veteran member of staff who was designated to wander around the plant looking for improvement opportunities.[26,27] These frontline leaders spend six dedicated months away from the assembly line to address issues that arise from their peers. "Kaizen men" are "selected for their leadership potential" and act as mentors to their peers until they have the skills needed to formally lead teams.[28] They succeed at problem solving closer to the issues and are the first responders to the Andon, a cable that is pulled to stop the assembly line and alert the team about an issue.

The "Kaizen man" is a first step toward the Lateral Leader as the Gemba incarnate but it has some shortcomings. First, the "Kaizen man" may become another layer of management to oversee work. The additional responsibilities and perception of leadership may lead to feelings of entitlement. Next, this model is costly and depends on high staffing levels, a luxury that is not afforded to every organization. Conservative staffing models leave little buffer for roles that are dedicated to improvement. And third, the "Kaizen man" no longer works directly on the production line, which means surrendering the status of "peer."[29] Losing this status means losing the full respect of the staff she once represented.

Imagine two engineers: one is a dedicated resource to education, completely removed from the work of engineering, and the other has a 50/50 contract between education and engineering. The former is responsible for proposing changes or improvements to engineers across the company. But no matter how valuable her proposed change is, the other engineers in the organization hold a deep skepticism of her ideas since she no longer practices engineering. On the other hand, the latter engineer receives notably less challenges from his peers. He still does the work, and the other engineers assume he would not propose a change that he himself would not benefit from. Although the two engineers have the same credentials, their level of respect from peers could not be further apart.

Looking Forward: The COVID-19 pandemic forced teams to adopt more electronic ways of communicating (Teams, Zoom, Slack, etc.). Frontline staff gained access to tools that functioned like social media in a work context. For once in history, the adoption of technology was no longer optional. It even outpaced technological development! Anyone could create a communal page where peers could pose questions, solve each other's problems, challenge standards, or simply lift each other up with humorous GIFs, memes, or photos. Peers became a click away, while managers remained a level removed. The entire Gemba shifted from a physical location to a digital playground.

Changes in our environment force us to challenge our deepest assumptions about work. Leaders in the post-pandemic work world must ask, "why do we continue to expect managers to solve the problems of staff when they do not understand the work?" As we have seen, organizations no longer have an excuse to rely on managers to support staff. Instead, peers must solve the problems of peers.

Based on logistics alone, the amount of time it takes for administrators to learn a process enough to ask good questions or escalate feedback is waste compared to the value-added time a Lateral Leader can spend at the heart of the matter. It is selfish for leaders to go to the Gemba for any reason other than forming relationships, gaining trust, or encouraging teams to work with their Lateral Leaders.[30] Lean literature must evolve out of its dependence on the physical Gemba. And systems must invest in Lateral Leaders, the Gemba incarnate.

Artisans

Primary Source: *Juran*

The master-apprentice relationship has existed since the earliest records of craft production and remains relevant in many modern professions. Woodworkers, plumbers, electricians, and many other fields of handiwork require hands-on learning. The master is like a sports coach giving a team a video of their game and letting them watch it "from behind."[31] Each relationship is based on our natural human tendency to seek out an individual for guidance who is further along in their journey to expertise. And apprentices, by their very existence, acknowledge the importance of journeying with others on our path to an improved process or a better outcome.

The medical field is also rife with master-apprentice relationships. They are hardcoded in the form of physician residency programs, clinical rotations, and precepting. It is almost impossible to become a doctor, advanced practice provider, or nurse without some sort of apprenticeship.

But the buck stops with the scrubs and rarely reaches the suits. Healthcare organizations seldom apply the same master-apprentice model to administrators or non-clinical frontline staff. This creates a training division between the two core roles in a healthcare organization. Sometimes, in its absence, administrative leaders apply the dyad model to team leadership, pairing a clinician with an administrator. Or they elevate clinicians into leadership positions. Each solution dances around an inevitable problem: non-clinical staff will *never* understand the clinic. And clinical staff, without education or experience, may struggle to understand the office. Without a wholesale switch to a dyad model, or the promotion of clinicians into leadership positions, we flounder between two very different models of work.

The Lateral Leader model provides one of the most cost-efficient and respectful models of partnership between suits and scrubs. Each Lateral Leader participates in two master-apprentice relationships: one with administration and another with their peers. Neither is a one-way street. And the relationship is mutually beneficial: Management can elicit feedback through the Lateral Leader to the frontline, and the Lateral Leader acts as a spokesperson of the frontline to management. She is a bi-directional translator who understands the business from both perspectives.

Two preconditions must first be met to enable this bi-directional relationship:

1. *Delegation* from leadership
2. *Trust* from the frontline

Juran says that leaders seeking culture change must *delegate* to "artisans" who "undergo an apprenticeship and thereby become qualified to practice a skilled trade as an independent craftsman."[32] He believes "the ideal of maximum delegation to the work force is largely attained in the case of the artisan."[33] Through delegation, leaders can multiply their impact and nurture talent closer to the frontline. To give the label of an artisan to an individual means allowing them the freedom of self-sufficiency.[34]

In an Empowerment System, managers should know *why* their staff complete a task, and a general understanding of *what* they do, but true delegation means being comfortable with not knowing *how* to complete the task. Thankfully, it is easier to ask managers to delegate to a Lateral Leader instead of blindly delegating to the frontline. The existence of Lateral Leaders can give the local manager an easy outlet when they do not know an answer. Instead of adding a question to their already lengthy to-do list, they can ask "have you asked your Lateral Leaders yet?" Here is some feedback from managers who have accepted the shift to delegation:

■ "I can finally focus on strategic thinking since I am no longer the firefighter for my staff."
■ "I used to think I had an advantage over my peer managers since I used to work at the frontline. Now I realize that I was getting in the way of peers helping each other when I use my experience to solve their problems for them."

Staff at the frontline must also *trust* the Lateral Leader. She is an extension of leadership but retains her most important quality: the same job title as her peers. In this role, she must keep a foot in two canoes, one in the frontline and one in leadership. Each organization must approach this balance in the way that befits their culture. Some companies pull the frontline staff away from their role to learn the tools and techniques of improvement before injecting them back into the system. ThedaCare in Wisconsin allows staff to spend a 6-month stint with full-time process coaches to learn the academic skills of Lean before returning to work.[35] They invest 6 months of nonproductive work to improve productivity down the line. Other systems offer periodic trainings or mentorship opportunities to invest in staff without hindering productivity. No matter the approach taken, the voice of the Lateral Leader must strike a balance between authentic support and unbiased criticism. Because the only thing worse than the outright failure to empower a team is giving the false hope of empowerment by listening to their voice and then failing to carry out the ideas submitted. Trust fades as authenticity fades. And perception rules the day. Staff must believe the Lateral Leader has their back.

The Lateral Leader, as an artisan, must be prepared to encounter distrust and resistance from both staff and leaders. She plays an important role in both master-apprentice relationships. On the one hand, frontline staff carry the baggage of empty promises made by leadership in the past. On the other, the words "Lean" or "Six Sigma" unearth past trauma that may ultimately hinder the adoption of a new system.[36] The term "empowerment" may become the next "flavor of the month" that is exciting for a time and later abandoned for another catchy word. It is critical, therefore, that the Lateral Leader, through trust and delegation, address the concerns head-on. She must dehumidify the air before it becomes stifling.

Internal Consultants

Primary Sources: *Imai, Toussaint*

The first question a leadership team asks when considering a process improvement transformation is "should we outsource this to a consultant or build this in house?" To answer this common "build or buy" question, we must understand the different options available:

1. Central management team (Build)
2. External consultants (Buy)
3. Internal consultants (Build)

A *central management team* is a department of project managers or process coaches, Black Belts or PMPs. This is a common route taken by companies that have the existing infrastructure to manage work in house. Each team is conscious of the local culture but is limited by the projects assigned to them by executive leaders. Their capacity is filled with a few discontinuous improvement projects that cross multiple value streams. And their success depends on their closeness to both top-level leadership and the frontline. It is common for one of these conditions to exist, but both is a luxury.

The central management team is limited by the individual strengths of its members, but it has the potential to become a powerful source of education for the rest of the organization. Many teams will offer Lean or Six Sigma training to employees to equip them with skills to use in their respective departments. The creation of curricula and execution of classes takes a significant investment of time and energy, with little feedback of success. Success is measured by volume of students taught instead of impact made, on the bottom line or the individual person. And the teachers cling to the hope that each student will carry the newfound skills into their departments.

The limitations of centralized project managers will often lead to the consideration of *external consultants*. Although consultants will present themselves differently, they all share a common goal: achieve profits for themselves and for the client (in that order) by applying a turnkey model. Unlike the central management team, it will take years for an external consultant to understand the culture of an organization enough to implement sustainable change.

But the easiest and most natural path to sustainable culture change is through the creation of "informal leaders among peers."[37] These *internal consultants* are frontline staff whose passion and interest in the work of improvement is ignited and stoked by a central management team while leveraging the disruptive methods of external consultants. They borrow the best elements of each without the cost or disruption. For example, the full-time members of the central management team are empowered to act as sensei to develop leaders among frontline staff without removing them from their stations like ThedaCare.[38] Education from a sensei is targeted and specialized, equipping the apprentice with helpful skills, and giving purpose to the master. And the corresponding feedback is immediate and personalized.

The internal consultant model is appealing to small central management teams who want to impact a large organization without needing to ask for additional resources in the form of staff. Internal consultants are both the cause and result of multiplication. Here, we continue to see the exponential effects of empowerment.

Sensors

Primary Sources: *Juran, Deming, Shingo, Training Within Industry (TWI)*

Planners and do-ers are like oil and water in the world of business operations. Construction designs from architects create tension with the contractors responsible for construction. Factory deadlines created by engineers produce tension with assembly line staff. Ideas can get lost in translation. Plans may overpromise an unrealistic outcome to a client. And without a *sensor*, the relationship between planners and do-ers will remain perpetually at odds.

Production systems owe this tension to the 20th-century philosophy of Taylorism, which relied on engineers to find and solve problems.[39] The image of an engineer standing behind assembly line staff with a stopwatch captures the core idea of Taylorism. Job Management (JM), one of the core elements of Training Within Industry (TWI) from the 1930s, challenged the underlying Tayloristic ideologies that ruled the factory floor. (The history of TWI will be covered in detail in chapter 6.) JM allowed supervisors, for the first time, to make changes without permission from the engineers.[40] This idea was revolutionary if we understand the context of the American economy at the time it was conceived: World War II. TWI was developed to train hundreds of thousands of civilians who had never held a factory job to fill the absence of the workers drafted into the war. In the absence of trained labor, TWI relied on frontline staff to detect problems before they had a negative impact on production. Like the supervisors in JM, our Lateral Leaders act as sensors in the Empowerment System.

Sensors must be built into a system to have the greatest impact. Consider this well-known example from Toyota: assembly line staff were originally placed in strategic locations around the factory to work on multiple machines at one time. Through a process of reflection, the workers and engineers discovered that many of the machines were random or unrelated in terms of a linear process. Staff felt less invested in the quality of a product if they worked on both the motor and the chassis at the same time. In response, they shifted the position of staff to multi-process handling across machines related to the same product. This change ensured staff were aware of how their decisions directly impacted the next process.[41]

Now imagine a doctor's office: The manager of the clinic observes how her registration staff are regularly skipping warnings during the registration, check-in, and check-out processes. The warnings were originally put in place to avoid issues with patient messaging, mailing, or billing. And the local manager is responsible for working the error work queues to follow behind their staff to fix any problems. During a routine meeting between the doctors, the manager, and the owner, it was discovered that an increased number of automated messages and bills had been sent to the wrong phone numbers and addresses. The owner applied pressure on the manager to reduce errors, which translated to pressure applied from management to the frontline staff. This classic example of top-down pressure to perform did not sit well with the Lateral Leaders among the staff. They explained to management how there were no perceived consequences of skipping errors since the impact was never felt at the front. The manager quickly realized how the sensor and the frontline worker were disconnected, and the impact was felt by all parties involved. Instead of suffering the unnecessary top-down pressures, the frontline staff asked for training on the error work queues. And, as a result, error rates decreased overnight. The owner was pleased, the frontline felt empowered, and management was removed from the tension. Although adoption continues to remain high, the local manager sometimes insists on managing the work queue on her own instead of delegating to the frontline workers. It is not surprising that these days have above-average error rates.

The Lateral Leader is the next part of a long answer to the question: "How do we reduce variation?" Many voices throughout the history of Lean have weighed in on the best methods to reduce variation, and the sensor is no exception. Each idea builds on or challenges the narrative that came before. First, Juran encouraged the use of audits to prevent variation. Inspectors visited workstations to watch staff with the standard work in hand. In contrast, Deming believed audits were the "equivalent to planning for defects."[42] A process without defects does not need inspection. Shingeo Shingo, an early engineer of the Toyota Production System, built on Deming's original criticism. He is known for his argument that inspectors at the end of an assembly line are waste since their very existence assumes the fact that errors are allowed in production. In response, Shingo developed an important Lean tool called Poka-Yoke, commonly translated as mistake proofing, to replace costly audits with sensors. Each part of the process has a sensor to catch errors at the source. From start to finish, our choice to include Lateral Leaders as sensors will lead to the "error proofing" of processes. With standard work and a voice, staff become "their own inspectors" to detect and reduce variation.[43] A final benefit of a sensor is to help improve standardization by detecting variation.[44]

Induction Educators

Primary Source: *Training Within Industry (TWI)*

The timelines of Lean consultants and central Improvement Teams will place education as the first step toward process transformation. They kick off an improvement program with training sessions for C-Suite and executive leaders to learn and drive changes from the top-down. And this is no haphazard choice. It is concrete and easy to quantify success by the number of bodies in chairs instead of processes impacted. A contract for a second year with the consultant is more easily justified. These same leaders then go on to manage their own projects, in addition to their previous work, and collectively pat each other on the back when they achieve results. As time goes on, education for management and the frontline happen last, assuming the program lasts long enough to reach them.

Education has a home in an improvement system, but not as the foundation. Let us draw upon pedagogical philosophy, or the study of education, to explain why.

It is wrong to assume that staff across the leadership continuum will benefit from the same type of education. What may be effective for one level of leadership is inappropriate for all levels. Recent developments in educational psychology explain how there are not learning styles in education as we always assumed (i.e., "I am a visual learner" or "I am a hands-on learner"). Rather, the *content* of the material is the driver for deciding which teaching medium is most appropriate. For example, mathematical content, which is difficult to express verbally, is best taught with hands-on or visual methods. Imaginative content, which is naturally artistic, is best taught audially or when read. The education of process improvement must evolve considering these findings.

Empowerment systems and production systems are action-based systems that require hands-on education because the *content* of improvement is experiential by nature. It is based on *induction*, a term first coined in TWI manuals.[45] Consider an induction cooktop compared to a traditional electric or gas range, or the technology that is used to wirelessly charge electronics (phones, toothbrushes, etc.). Induction does not use an outside source of energy such as an electric heating element or the combustion of natural gas. Instead, electricity is generated by a magnetic field inside of the source (stove, charger, etc.) which is then transmitted into a piece of metal inside of the object (pan, phone, toothbrush). Induction is touted as more efficient and faster than external energy transfer since the energy stays within the heated object instead of flowing around it. It is also safer since energy transfer requires contact and does not happen when the objects are separated.

Language is an excellent example of education by means of induction. It is the bridge between education and culture. And it helps to differentiate one culture from neighboring cultures. We saw this addressed above, where popular Lean programs will first educate leaders on the common words and phrases to use when discussing improvement. We must share a common vernacular to make sense of the world around us. Now this seems like a reasonable use of linear thinking until we consider a lateral alternative: slang. In schools, students organically learn and share slang terms that are part of the common vernacular. Many slang terms are a shortened or simplified version of a formal word that expresses a depth of meaning and creates a distinct community between those who use it. They are easily learned in context but require explanation out of context. A teenager may have difficulty explaining to her parents the exact definition of a new slang term, but at school it simply makes sense. Consider "bet" as an affirming exclamation or response – it is synonymous with "groovy" (1970s-80s) or "cool" (1990s-2010s) when used in conversation but makes little sense out of context. Similarly, the word "sus," a shortened version of "suspicious" or "suspect," captures depth with brevity. It quickly describes a complex reality without going into much detail. In all slang, formality and being "right" is replaced by cultural infectiousness.

Lean is most effective when it is embodied in the slang of the culture, not when it is called "Lean." For example, teenage slang loses its allure when it is appropriated by adults or used in commercial marketing. The organic and self-organizing qualities of corporate slang must also remain part of the unwritten language of the system without being codified. Leaders can use it in dialogue, but not formal documentation.

In conclusion, the leadership expert, Peter Senge, argues how we must integrate learning and working.[46] The induction educator is modeled off of the "master trainer" in TWI who trained other staff and paved the way for modern "train the trainer" models.[47] They focused 95% of time on the job training and 5% on formal education.[48] This notion is consistently reinforced in contemporary Lean literature: "In fact, our experience has been that the best trainers are those who have little or no training experience, but a deep background in the industry and jobs in which they are working."[49] Here we see how Lean, in addition to being an empowerment system, is also an "education system."[50] The guidebooks from TWI reiterate this in a question: "How do you create a culture that empowers the hourly worker? Training."[51]

Lean systems should avoid classroom training in favor of hands-on education because, in the words of Liker, "It is easier to act your way to a new way of thinking than think your way to a new way of acting."[52] Although leaders are predisposed to learn hands-on content in a written or audible way, a day spent shadowing a Lateral Leader is the best classroom. The education of slang is best led by the Lateral Leader, a form of induction within the workplace. She is responsible for translating slang for leadership while channeling strategy to the frontline. And she does so at the appropriate time, not always at the beginning.

The Job of Lateral Leaders

We have explored the various titles the Lateral Leader has been given across the history of Lean. She has gone by many names, including:

- Change Agents
- Attractors
- Experienced Amateurs
- The Gemba Incarnate
- Artisans
- Internal Consultants
- Sensors
- Induction Educators

We now turn from theory to application. The Lateral Leader has a few core responsibilities, regardless of the organization:

- Review ideas submitted by peers.
- Respond to questions from peers.
- Partner one-on-one with new hires.
- Participate in ad hoc projects as a representative of their role.

Each Lateral Leader commits somewhere between 1-1.5 years as a Lateral Leader before passing the voluntary mantle to another peer. Compare this with ThedaCare that cycles managers through the central Improvement Team for 2 years to grow as Lean leaders.[53] Alternatively, Toyota cycles the "Kaizen man" every 6 months.[54] Our recommendation of 18 months comes directly from the feedback of Lateral Leaders who expressed how they had given all they could at the 18-month mark. Although more of a good thing is tempting, any further time would result in diminishing returns.

It is also tempting to promote the Lateral Leader into a "Team Leader" role with a meager pay increase. The introduction of a new job code can hardcode the culture of improvement into a Human Resource (HR) system and add a new rung to the ladder of career development. But it will limit culture change. Less people will have the opportunity to learn by induction. The opportunity cost is far greater than the short-term benefit. Again, this decision was supported by actual Lateral Leaders when given the option: "Would you rather permanently become Lateral Leaders, with a small pay increase, or give other peers the opportunity to be a Lateral Leader?" Time and time again, the decision is unanimous: Lateral Leaders would rather let their peers be part of the improvement process instead of locking down a promotion. Empowered staff empower others.

As we continue to see, extrinsic motivators are inappropriate for Lateral Leaders. Organizations must instead discern the most appropriate forms of intrinsic motivation to invest back in these staff. *Leadership development* and *mentorship* are two effective offerings that both motivate and advance the workforce. Consider a line worker, scheduler, or hygienist these budding leaders would not otherwise be given the opportunity to have a mentor from the leadership team or be offered classes on leadership skills. Organizations often reserve such offerings for managers and above, not frontline staff. But imagine a workforce of frontline staff who are driven by their desires to improve their skills in public speaking or small group facilitation instead of chasing a financial bonus. We must always remember that the goal of an Empowerment System is to equip and invest in the future leaders of the organization, not buy them.

Recall that an Empowerment System, by focusing first on the untapped potential of staff, and second on improvement, will outperform traditional Lean Production Systems that focus first on improvement. In a similar way, the promotion of Lateral Leaders is a secondary goal to personal development, but it remains noteworthy. In one organization, 24% of Lateral Leaders were promoted from their role either during or after their 18-month rotation. The culture of this organization has even grown accustomed to interviewing Lateral Leaders before considering other internal or external candidates. The goal of a Lean Empowerment System is to make it hard for leaders to choose between multiple experienced and emotionally intelligent candidates who are a product of the very culture they seek to improve. An organization is bound for success when the leaders outnumber leadership positions.

The Process Improvement Team

Lateral Leaders encounter success when the system is predisposed toward success. As we discussed in Chapter 4, the leadership team is responsible for creating the right guardrails to spark the influx of ideas. Each guardrail moves a system closer to the construction of a home for the Lateral Leaders. It is then the role of staff to issue a prudent response. They must feel comfortable to learn and grow as "amateurs," while being pushed slightly outside of their comfort zone. Here we introduce the Process Improvement Team as the stage where the Lateral Leaders act and learn.

The Process Improvement Team is generically named because its real identity will morph depending on its members. Every 18-month cycle has a new face and personality. The Process Improvement Team was originally designed as a collaboration between operational leadership, technical support, and frontline staff and must include the players who can quickly make or escalate an idea to the right team for approval or denial. Each role fills in the missing context of the next. The only way the pace of improvement can match the rate of ideas from the frontline is by reducing waste and rework in the system. Increased colocation (digitally or in person) and better management of ideas (accountability and task tracking) will inevitably lead to increased results. But many improvement systems fail to sustain due to a lack of cadence and accountability. A team cannot simply meet for a full day value-mapping or a full week Rapid Improvement Event (RIE) and expect sustainable returns. They must instead embrace the virtues of regimentation, meeting on a regular cadence, addressing any issue, no matter how small, and slowing down to match the organic pace of improvement.[55]

Let us explore the role of each member of the Process Improvement Team:

- **Lateral Leaders**: They have their ears to their peers and speak on their behalf like the Electoral College in American politics.
- **Operations Team**: The work of improvement is sometimes shielded from the human resource tensions, management foibles, or local problems that exist. The operations leaders must provide the local context of the Lateral Leaders for the rest of the Process Improvement Team. They understand the political atmosphere and potential impacts of a decision and can therefore provide insight into the departments where Lateral Leaders are pulled. Finally, the operations leaders can make the

rest of the Process Improvement Team aware of potential Lateral Leaders or provide feedback on members who may need additional coaching prior to becoming a member of the Process Improvement Team.

■ **Education Team**: The Process Improvement Team becomes a new home for the training materials and standards of each role. Some education teams may view the existence of a Process Improvement Team as a threat to their role. But it is important to emphasize how the Process Improvement Team can provide a streamlined means of documenting, partnering, and communicating changes as a supplement to the training team, not a replacement.

■ **Technical Team**: The inclusion of a member from the IT department or electronic medical record (EMR) team has reciprocal benefits for both the member and the team. New ideas from frontline staff are quickly reviewed by the technical team for feasibility and impact on ancillary systems. The technical team can also bring forward any idea or ticket that was opened by a staff member outside of the Process Improvement Team for review by Lateral Leaders. A two-way street is formed that can add value to both departments. The weekly meeting becomes the single and only funnel for all ideas pertaining to the role in question, making sure that resources are committed to the right work at the right time.

■ **Process Coach**: The role of the central improvement team changes from a "master builder" project manager to a coach, facilitator, and guide. The process coach is responsible for organizing and managing the administrative duties that allow the team to focus on improvements. She is also viewed as an expert in facilitation instead of being viewed as just another role. These facilitators "hold the context" of dialogue.[56] They act in a similar way to the internal consultant, helping peers solve the problems of peers as a third-party observer.

■ **Other Roles**: As the Process Improvement Team matures, the process coach can delegate her administrative tasks to the Lateral Leaders. Each delegation helps the group become more sustainable as the process coach moves from facilitator to mentor. It also helps teach the Lateral Leaders important leadership skills they may otherwise not have the chance to practice in their role.

In this chapter we have argued in favor of lateral thinking as opposed to linear thinking. Tiered systems are inferior to parallel systems. The influence of Lateral Leaders is greater than that of elected leaders. And we must replace our obsession with solutions with a devotion to learning. In the spirit of learning, we looked back throughout the history of Lean to identify our Lateral Leader by her many names. She is our primary companion on the journey to improvement and the embodiment of lateral thinking.

The Lateral Leader is the missing piece of the Lean puzzle and the key to the Lean Empowerment System. Empowerment needs a figurehead who is at the same time source, creator, and recipient of change. She participates in both the microsystem and macrosystem, encouraging by her very existence the challenges of self-organization and organic development. She is a microcosm of improvement, a dynamic human system, and a translator between the frontline and leadership. And she is a daily reminder for leaders to balance the pillars of continuous improvement and respect for people.

Energy courses through her every move. The *energy of improvement*, as opposed to the energy of empowerment, follows the first law of thermodynamics. This is known as conservation of energy: energy is not created or destroyed but transferred from one body to another. The energy of improvement is not created out of thin air. Less cannot make more, only the same, or less. Veins of creative energy are rare in the world of improvement.

Empowerment energy, on the other hand, breaks the second law of thermodynamics. It is like nuclear fusion, which can create the phenomenon of "ignition" where *less* can make *more*. One measure of energy input can result in two measures of energy output. The first successful occasion of ignition took place in December 2022 resulting in 154% energy yield.[57] An injection of energy multiplies instead of entropies. But this requires a stable system where particles can collide without loss. A powerful laser heats a small sphere, causing an implosion at hundreds of millions of degrees. The conditions must be perfect, or the untamed energy may result in catastrophic outcomes. In a similar way, we must first tap into the energy of empowerment, then channel it into the work of improvement.

The next stop on our journey through the Lean Empowerment System is Process. The common ideas of Kaizen, Suggestion Systems, and Standard Work will be transformed in the presence of the Lateral Leader and her Process Improvement Team. Reframing our telos away from efficiency and toward people will remove process improvement from the spotlight. It is no longer the end, but a means to a greater end. I hope you will see process ideas in a new light once the burden of expectation placed by Lean Production Systems is lifted off leaders and shared on the shoulders of Lateral Leaders.

Notes

1 Gossiping is a way staff show you they feel like they don't have a voice, from Ron Friedman, *The Best Place to Work: The Art and Science of Creating an Extraordinary Workplace* (Los Angeles, CA: Tarcher Perigee, 2015), 126.

2 Push and Pull communication are both examples of linear thinking. Push refers to active message styles like emails, memos, and newsletters, where leaders take ideas and push them to the frontline. Pull, on the other hand, requires a central repository of information which is updated by leaders and staff can passively access the source as needed. But, both of these models still assume that communication is required between the leader and the frontline staff.

3 Based on Training Within Industry – 26 – "Train industrial people to handle their own problems."

4 Peter Senge, *The Fifth Discipline* (Manhattan, NY: Random House Business, 2006), 136.

5 Emily Adams and John Toussaint, *Management on the Mend: The Healthcare Executive Guide to System Transformation* (Appleton, WI: ThedaCare Center for Healthcare Value, 2015), 142.

6 Ibid.

7 Brenda Zimmerman, Curt Lindberg, and Paul Plsek, *Edgeware: Lessons from Complexity Science for Health Care Leaders* (Irving, Texas V H A, Incorporated, 2008), 80–81.

8 Robert Miller, *Hearing the Voice of the Shingo Principles: Creating Sustainable Cultures of Enterprise Excellence* (Abingdon, Oxfordshire: Routledge, 2018), 47.

9 Emily Adams and John Toussaint, *Management on the Mend: The Healthcare Executive Guide to System Transformation* (Appleton, WI: ThedaCare Center for Healthcare Value, 2015), 141.

10 Timothy R. Clark, *The 4 Stages of Psychological Safety: Defining the Path to Inclusion and Innovation* (Oakland, CA: Berrett-Koehler Publishers, Inc., 2020), 72.

11 Ibid., 103.

12 Amy C. Edmondson, *The Fearless Organization: Creating Psychological Safety in the Workplace for Learning, Innovation, and Growth* (Hoboken, NJ: John Wiley & Sons, 2019), 105.

13 Brenda Zimmerman, Curt Lindberg, and Paul Plsek, *Edgeware: Lessons from Complexity Science for Health Care Leaders* (Irving, Texas V H A, Incorporated, 2008), 80–81.

14 De Bono believes attractors are a negative thing in systems since they attract more of what has come before. I disagree since they are peers and instill comfort and safety, the prerequisites for improvement (see Edward De Bono, *Lateral Thinking: Creativity Step by Step* (New York, NY: Harper Perennial, 1990)).

15 Frances Westley, Brenda Zimmerman, & Michael Patton, *Getting to Maybe: How the World is Changed* (Toronto, ON: Vintage Canada, 2007), 38.

16 Ibid., 60, 37.

17 Donald Dinero, *Training Within Industry: The Foundation of Lean* (New York, NY: Productivity Press, 2005), 205.

18 Shingeo Shingo, *A Study of the Toyota Production System* (Boca Raton, FL: Routledge, 1989), xxvi.

19 J. M. Juran, *Juran on Leadership for Quality: An Executive Handbook* (Florence, MA: Free Press, 1989), 84.

20 Walter A. Shewart, *Statistical Method from the Viewpoint of Quality Control* (Mineola, NY: Dover Publications, 1986), i.

21 Daniel Kahneman, Olivier Sibony, and Cass R. Sunstein, *Noise: A Flaw in Human Judgment* (Boston, MA: Little, Brown Spark, 2021), 226.

22 Walter A. Shewart, *Statistical Method from the Viewpoint of Quality Control* (Mineola, NY: Dover Publications, 1986), ii.

23 Tom Peters and Bob Waterman, *In Search of Excellence: Lessons from America's Best-Run Companies* (New York, NY: Harper Business, 2006).

24 Daniel Markovitz, *Building the Fit Organization: Six Core Principles for Making Your Company Stronger, Faster, and More Competitive* (New York: McGraw-Hill Education, 2016), 102.

25 In healthcare, it is widely known that administrators do not generate revenue for the organization. There are very few staff who do not wear scrubs that directly impact cash flow.

26 Masaaki Imai, *Kaizen (ky'zen): The Key to Japan's Competitive Success* (New York City, NY: McGraw-Hill, 1991), 96.

27 I will use the phrase "man" as a direct quote from Imai.

28 Jeffrey K. Liker and George Trachilis, *Developing Lean Leaders at All Levels: A Practical Guide* (Jacksonville, FL: Lean Leadership Institute Publications, 2014), 176.

29 Ibid., 177.

30 We will continue to redefine the role of a manager in the presence of Lateral Leaders in a later chapter.

31 Shingeo Shingo, *A Study of the Toyota Production System* (Boca Raton, FL: Routledge, 1989), 146.

32 J. M. Juran, *Juran on Leadership for Quality: An Executive Handbook* (Florence, MA: Free Press, 1989), 264.

33 Ibid.

34 Ibid.

35 Emily Adams and John Toussaint, *Management on the Mend: The Healthcare Executive Guide to System Transformation* (Appleton, WI: ThedaCare Center for Healthcare Value, 2015), 79.

36 The Empowerment System avoids using the titles "Lean" or Six Sigma" due to the stigmas among staff and management. The term "empowerment" is still commonly accepted as a positive goal.

37 Masaaki Imai, *Kaizen (ky'zen): The Key to Japan's Competitive Success* (New York City, NY: McGraw-Hill, 1991), 217.

38 Michael Ballé and D. T. Jones, *The Lean Sensei: Go See Challenge* (Boston, MA: Lean Enterprise Institute, 2019), 49.

39 Donald Dinero, *Training Within Industry: The Foundation of Lean* (New York, NY: Productivity Press, 2005), 50, 124.

40 Ibid., 127.

41 Shingeo Shingo, *A Study of the Toyota Production System* (Boca Raton, FL: Routledge, 1989), 157.

42 W. Edwards Deming, *Out of the Crisis* (Cambridge, MA: The MIT Press, 2018), 11.

43 Thomas L. Jackson, *Standard Work for Lean Healthcare (Lean Tools For Healthcare Series)* (New York, NY: Productivity Press, 2011), 82.

44 J. M. Juran, *Managerial Breakthrough* (New York, NY: McGraw-Hill Book Co., 1995), 194.

45 Donald Dinero, *Training Within Industry: The Foundation of Lean* (New York, NY: Productivity Press, 2005), 282.

46 Peter Senge, *The Fifth Discipline* (Manhattan, NY: Random House Business, 2006), 287.

47 Donald Dinero, *Training Within Industry: The Foundation of Lean* (New York, NY: Productivity Press, 2005), 68.

48 Ibid., 31.

49 Patrick Graupp and Martha Purrier, *Getting to Standard Work in Health Care: Using TWI to Create a Foundation for Quality Care* (New York, NY: Productivity Press, 2022), 162.

50 Michael Ballé and D. T. Jones, *The Lean Sensei: Go See Challenge* (Boston, MA: Lean Enterprise Institute, 2019), 2.

51 Donald Dinero, *Training Within Industry: The Foundation of Lean* (New York, NY: Productivity Press, 2005), xviii.

52 Jeffrey K. Liker & George Trachilis, *Developing Lean Leaders at All Levels: A Practical Guide* (Jacksonville, FL: Lean Leadership Institute Publications, 2014), 164–65.

53 Emily Adams and John Toussaint, *Management on the Mend: The Healthcare Executive Guide to System Transformation* (Appleton, WI: ThedaCare Center for Healthcare Value, 2015), 141.

54 Masaaki Imai, *Kaizen (ky'zen): The Key to Japan's Competitive Success* (New York City, NY: McGraw-Hill, 1991).

55 Atul Gawande, *The Checklist Manifesto* (New York, NY: Picador), 162.

56 Peter Senge, *The Fifth Discipline* (Manhattan, NY: Random House Business, 2006), 226.

57 https://en.wikipedia.org/wiki/National_Ignition_Facility

Chapter 6

Process

Empowerment System Definition:
A self-organizing body of Lateral Leaders *who improve Standard Work in a Kaizen Suggestion System*

Ponder the question: "Can a large organization be a true democracy?"
  Now consider a string of follow-up questions:

- Is it possible to release power to the people, or do some choices need to be made at the top?
- Does everyone *truly* have a voice, or do we just create the illusion of choice to improve culture?
- Can empowerment *really* exist?

The answers to these questions are not simple. They demand years of system development, human investment, and leadership alignment. Leaders must not only care enough to ask them but remain humble enough to hear the answers.

Instead of tackling the questions head-on, let us start with a thought experiment. We can expand our understanding of business when we observe it through the lens of American democracy.

Although governments are not businesses, they share some core symbolic elements, namely, the healthy tension between federal (macro) and state (micro) control. Sometimes we see this split up geographically, by tax codes or counties. Other times the lines are demarcated by walls and doors

 DOI: 10.4324/9781032644134-9

between departments in a building. And now, with the advent of remote work, organizational charts are no longer the source of truth for illustrating the flow of influence in an organization. But no matter the physical structure, layout, or reporting structure of an organization, we experience an age-old tension between global and local, or *federal* and *state* levels.

The current two-party American political system tends to split emphasis between federal control (Democratic Party) or state control (Republican Party). We will remain nonpartisan for the sake of our discussion here and consider the reasons why both models are valuable. Just as our government would fail to exist without both, a company would suffer grave outcomes if it were to ignore one level or the other.

First, federal systems give every person a voice (vote), but it is management that hears it, not peers. Value can be lost in translation as data flows vertically instead of laterally. And the sheer volume of voices in a federal system can also result in inaction. The system is smothered by the weight of ideas and suffers analysis paralysis. Or, in the attempt to shake paralysis and *do something*, a system might emphasize the ideas of the loudest voices, or the voices of those who chose to speak, neglecting those who did not, at that moment, speak. Each big idea draws the attention of big money, and lobbyists meddle with the organic development of ideas. All these possible scenarios can be summarized thus: the best idea doesn't always win. The opportunities for distrust are frequent. And any ounce of distrust in the system will further limit the number of staff that feel comfortable floating their voice into the political arena, thus creating a vicious cycle with each political cycle.

Despite the possible shortcomings, the federal level does succeed in providing a safety net when the state level is unequipped to respond appropriately. It is a check and balance to the messiness of human behavior that can overtake organic systems. Yet the level of clarity demanded in the global arena is only attainable when leadership promotes a unifying message that resonates with the people. For this, it must remain tapped into the lateral flow of thinking among peers. This exists at the local level.

The local state level is more than just the *Gemba*, where the work happens. It is the nucleus of community, like the family unit. Recall the idea of subsidiarity from Chapter 1 – the local level respects the smallest form of community and creates structures where it may flourish. Each idea, rumor, complaint, and opinion are formed at this level, conceived in the heart of a single person. Then the responsibility to deliver and foster an improvement falls to the community. It takes a village.

But, because of our human nature, tensions and even crimes between individuals arise out of unresolved conflicts or systemic pressures. People disagree about what is an improvement and what is not. Unlikely teams form around fringe ideas. Or truly valuable ideas play second fiddle to ideas backed by money or a charismatic leader. The growth of a community, therefore, is limited by the very people who seek to improve it. Our local systems can only aspire to reach a state of self-sustainability if they can facilitate dialogue between people and leadership while self-enforcing against unnecessarily combative behavior. This is an honorable feat that even the most talented and equipped Lateral Leader will struggle to facilitate. Each team may foster its own culture and identity, potentially in tension with or defined as "self-against" the system. Or ideas arise and swirl in a sea of peers without an advocate who can initiate true change. Improvements may not be heard if left to the devices of local leadership, or successful results of experimentation may not reach other teams who could benefit from the ideas.

In the end, our nation is built on this healthy tension, albeit messy, between local and federal governments. And in a similar way, an Empowerment System must contain a balance between the two. The Lateral Leaders resemble the Electoral College, hearing the voice of the people and casting their vote on behalf of the state.

Now we must break from the patriotic metaphor and explore not the birth of a nation, but the birth of an idea. Elections in the Lean Empowerment System do not produce new officials. They instead turn ideas into standards, standards into complaints, and complaints into more ideas. And so goes the virtuous cycle of the Empowerment Dream.

This chapter will draw upon systems theory (System) and Lateral Leaders (People) to frame an introduction of our third element, Process. We will start with a comparison of Kaizen and Innovation, two common methods for improvement. Then we will introduce the common Suggestion System through both old and new lenses: Training Within Industry (TWI), psychological safety, and contemporary theories of motivation. After the stage is set, we will transition into a comprehensive analysis of Standard Work and Standard Work for leaders, striking an important and often overlooked distinction between how to write standard work (SDCA) and how to improve standard work (PDCA). Now the real work of improvement begins.

Kaizen

Change: From Kai to Zen, and Back Again

Change management is one of the most challenging parts of process improvement. The process of change is often perceived as uncomfortable for both the agent of change and those impacted. At one extreme, it is a "creative destruction" where "assumptions need to be exposed and re-examined in light of changing needs and environments."[1] Or it is so small and mundane that those impacted pay little notice. No matter the scope or breadth, change is a paradox of human nature that keeps atrophy at bay.

Kaizen is commonly defined as "rapid improvement," but the literal etymology tells a far richer story. In Japanese, "Kai" is translated as change. The second half of the word, "Zen," is common in pop culture since it has been appropriated into the English language. It translates to "right state."[2] Practitioners of meditation pursue a Zen-like state of peace and awareness of their surroundings. It is not too dissimilar to the "right time" of Kairos introduced in Chapter 4.

Kai and Zen reflect the two universal seasons of life and death (Introduction). And the word Kaizen invites us to hold them in a difficult tension. Find stability, then change. Stabilize again, simply to change again, and so on. Set your feet long enough to launch to the next idea.

This is unlike our common understanding of change. We view change as chaos, and stability as stagnancy, or, even worse, complacency. But control over Zen gives us control over Kai.[3] The Zen in Kaizen gives clear direction from where one is changing (Kai) and the goal of where we hope to land (Zen). The starting point of a change is half of the story, simply leaving the end point unknown. In the words of Charles Kettering, famous inventor, and namesake of the major Ohio medical network, "A problem well stated is a problem half-solved." The "right state" of Zen is both the desired starting point and end point of Kai, change. It is where people gather.

Masaaki Imai introduces his book on Kaizen with a profoundly simple contrast between Kaizen and Innovation. He argues that Western companies rely on innovation for breakthroughs whereas Eastern companies prefer Kaizen. Innovation refers to massive, result-oriented changes. Kaizen includes small scale and rapid changes that are process-oriented.[4] Kaizen happens inside the box, whereas innovation thinks outside of the box. Kaizen is *ongoing* and involves *everyone*, not just leadership who are privy to innovation.[5] Yet, in the words of Imai, "both innovation and kaizen are needed if a company is to survive and grow."[6] Although contemporary Lean practitioners tend to focus primarily on discontinuous innovation projects, a Lean Empowerment System must strike a balance between the two and place a heavy emphasis on Kaizen.

Suggestion System

A suggestion system is a funnel for both innovation and Kaizen. Though, it is unfortunate that the most popular example of a suggestion system is also the least effective. The anonymous "Suggestion Box" screwed into the wall of restaurant lobbies and workplace break rooms is supposed to symbolize empowerment. It screams "you have a voice!" but fails to explain what will happen to your ballot once it enters the box. There are more questions than answers: Does anyone really read these? How will I know if my idea leads to change? What if they need more information about my idea? The box gives each customer a cathartic pillow to yell into and lets management get off the hook for doing the hard work of improvement. It appears harmless until we consider what is missing.

At its best, a suggestion system is a feedback loop that elicits feedback from a customer.[7] It starts with the shared experience of a process or a documented standard. Leadership then invites the customer to provide a suggestion, either constructive or not, to change the source of truth. Someone with the power or authority to make a change will field the suggestions, prioritize what is possible, and execute accordingly. The standard is then updated based on the suggestions, starting the loop all over again.

But the suggestion system has baggage. Mark Graban, in *Healthcare Kaizen*, explains how a traditional suggestion system is riddled with administrative overhead and remains heavily dependent on management. For example, ideas often end up in the hands of a manager, "getting added to the manager's long list of tasks. Since managers are typically very busy people, with other higher-priority items regularly popping up, an idea often gets buried in the pile."[8] He continues to drive in his point, explaining how this should have never been the result: "Kaizen emphasizes implementing most ideas or, at the least, giving timely and collaborative feedback to every employee who has an idea, not just those that are deemed accepted by a far-off committee."[9] But time after time we see suggestion systems that lapse into management dependence, a choice that is, in the end, self-defeating. The number of skeptics grows as the number of ideas gathers dust.

But all is not lost. A suggestion system can be redeemed by plugging a sensor into the feedback loop. For background, a traditional feedback loop in psychology goes from Signal ➔ Sensor ➔ Controller ➔ Effector ➔ Signal, and so on.[10] The sensor, introduced in our chapter on the Lateral Leader (Ch 5), is nestled into the system to sense the concentration of a signal and transmit that information to the controller. It removes the common tendency to add a task for a manager's approval since it is closest to the signal.[11] Like Poka-Yoke, it error proofs a suggestion system and empowers with a human touch.

Juran, in his book *Juran on Leadership for Quality*, provides a helpful introduction to suggestion systems that makes a case for their revival. He explains how, at their basic level, "suggestion systems have intrinsic merit because they provide workers with an opportunity to participate in creative activity."[12] And, like the Empowerment System, it must regard each worker as an expert.[13] The system must place its trust in the staff closest to the work and elicit ways to make it better. Juran goes on to break down the positive impact of a suggestion system into three key categories:

1. A shorter feedback loop and thereby an earlier response to quality problems
2. A greater sense of participation and ownership by the workforce
3. Liberation of managers from much delegable work[14]

The following section is a comprehensive overview of the suggestion system. It is split into three sections: the history, the context, and the impact of suggestion systems. We will start our analysis with the history of the suggestion system as it grew out of Training Within Industry. Next on our journey is the important context for the genesis of suggestions, namely, psychological safety in a system. A brief exploration into this discipline will reveal how critical an atmosphere for safety is for suggestions to arise. Third, we will define the impact of suggestion systems and lay out the quantification of improvement. And finally, we will offer a warning to any system designer who uses rewards to motivate staff into submitting suggestions.

The History: TWI (Training Within Industry)

We briefly introduced the history of TWI on a few occasions throughout this book (Ch 3 and 5). To recap, TWI was the first national program in the United States to propose a systematically "right way" to do a task beyond the recommendation of masters to apprentices.[15] It was a teaching method-ology used by the American government to educate an entirely new work-force to the factory floor after much of the previous workers were drafted into the military.

The TWI model is commonly broken into three programs: Job Instruction (JI), Job Relations (JR), and Job Methods (JM). JI included the basic stan-dards and breakdown of a task. JR improved the human dimension of work and taught ways to reduce tensions between workers. And JM leveraged the human potential developed in JR to improve the standards in JI. To those familiar with process improvement, this progression is reminiscent of the most basic forms of PDCA, Kaizen, or Lean improvement. Masaaki Imai even goes as far to argue how *the modern suggestion system came from TWI*.[16] It was born out of desperation and changed the entire industry.

Since then, almost every organization has learned that systematic change is either caused by choice or necessity. In this case, the war effort forced the TWI programs into existence. Managers were scantly more experienced than the workers, which removed the dependence on experienced manag-ers by force. Companies had no choice but to allow the people generating ideas to be the implementers of those ideas. In a similar way, the majority of companies resisted remote work for decades before switching systems overnight in the face of the COVID-19 pandemic. They shifted less out of choice than desperation. But some forward-thinking organizations had championed these ideas out of choice well before others were forced into it. Whether change comes from necessity or by choice is not as important as that which remains in the culture as time goes on. TWI showed us the sticking power of empowerment, and it is hard to close our eyes once they have been opened.

The Context: Psychological Safety

Since TWI our society has progressed leaps and bounds, especially in the field of psychology. A chapter about change in the modern workplace would be incomplete if we did not explore motivation and the context of safety. Safety is a prerequisite for people to engage in the process of change. And no suggestion system will work without it.[17]

A handful of voices in the psychological community have addressed the topic of psychological safety. Baer defines a climate of psychological safety as: "formal and informal organizational practices and procedures guiding and supporting open and trustful interactions within the work

environment."[18] Alfie Kohn explains how people actually need uncondi-
tional approval and acceptance.[19] And most pointedly, Clark admonishes
that "if we don't offer psychological safety, we're choosing to value something higher than human beings."[20] Each one of us has experienced psychological safety, or lack thereof, and can recognize its inherent privilege in the
workplace. But we are just starting to learn the role it plays in change
management.[21]

The reality of our situation is bleak: *improvement will not happen without psychological safety*. A study of process improvement in German companies showed that only the ones with psychological safety had higher
performance after implementing process improvements.[22] The research
went as far to illustrate how "innovation paired with a low level of climate
for initiative may negatively effect company performance."[23] Launching a
process improvement program without first establishing a climate of psychological safety is bound to backfire, no matter how charismatic the leader
or tried and true the model. Safety is the prerequisite for success, and it is
held by staff.

But the path to safety is long and rarely taken. Frontline staff have accu-
mulated years of distrust and skepticism from programs that have come and
gone as the "flavor of the month." Their first response to a new program
will likely match their skepticism. A recent study on psychological safety
and motivation details the three most common responses that students use
when given the opportunity to use their voice in the classroom.[24] The same
three responses can be observed in a workplace where psychological safety
is absent: escapism, exaggeration, and flattery.

1. **Escapism**: The first response is an "escape from freedom" as staff
   denounce the work of improvement. We hear this view in the following expressions: "Someone is responsible, but not me! I can hardly do
   my job, let alone make it better. That is above my pay grade." Staff
   who espouse this way of thinking are an opportunity cost in hiding.
   According to Miller, "we are wasting all of the untapped potential of
   the employee" if they remain this way.[25]
2. **Exaggeration**: The second response is the use of obviously inappropriate suggestions to see if the leader reasserts authority in the face of
   absurdity. Staff use this tactic to try and confirm their suspicions
   about the gesture being inauthentic. They test the water with purposefully antagonistic statements to poke and prod until gaps become
   visible.

3. **Flattery**: And third, people will say what they assume the leader wants to hear. They may be anxious to please. Or they don't fully trust that the leader wants to hear what they will say. Or they are simply ignorant because no one has helped them think through the decision-making process before. No matter the cause, it is tempting for the leader to accept hearing what they want to hear. We all like being right. We all want others to agree with us. But this is a delusion. We have not achieved empowerment.

Consider psychological safety in a similar way to statistical control theory; is your system stable enough to propose dramatic changes? Or are you still receiving responses of escapism, exaggeration, or flattery? A system must attain the state of control before injecting change.[26] In an Empowerment System, the foundation of psychological safety is laid by the Lateral Leaders before proposing change. We recognize that no system has a perfect climate of psychological safety, and perfection cannot be the nemesis of initiative. So we must succumb to building the plane of safety as we fly, knowing our co-pilots are the most important part of the plane. They will guide us through the turbulence and into a climate of psychological safety. The journeyers are more important than both the journey and the destination, and the only way to enjoy the fruits of either.

The Data: Quantifying Improvement

Politicians ask themselves the same question every election cycle: every citizen has a vote, but many do not use it. Why? What more must we do?

The purpose of this section is to use data to answer a similar set of questions: "Why do some people choose to *not* use their voice in an improvement system? Why don't people submit ideas to a suggestion system?"

Let us first set a baseline. According to a Gallup poll, only 30% of staff believe they have a voice at work.[27] And we can further whittle down this number to 15% who represent the over-achievers, engaged staff, or youthful optimists who participate in any managerial experiment (Referenced below as "+"). We see this plainly illustrated by "participative management," an early example of empowerment, where the average number of staff who participated was less than 15%.[28] Then another 15% are the detractors who are actively disengaged and complain about initiatives for change (Referenced below as "-"). And the final 70% are the skeptics straddling the

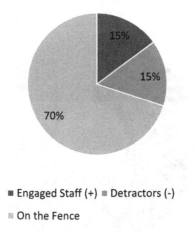

Figure 6.1 Categories of staff.

fence (Figure 6.1). Some believe they have a voice, and others are more skeptical. Their vote can swing under the right influence.

We must be clear as we set out on our mathematical musings: the goal of the Empowerment System is staff knowing they have a voice and how to use it, with idea generation as secondary. We must accept the unpopular opinion that our goal is not to engage all frontline staff. It is unrealistic to seek such a lofty goal.

So let us play out the scenario of engagement efforts in a traditional Lean Production System and in a Lean Empowerment System. Refer to Figures 6.2 and 6.3 as we go. The participative staff (15%) are system agnostic; they are motivated to engage in a new process out of personal interest in career development or an internal drive to succeed. The detractors (15%) will refuse to engage since Lean Production looks like and smells like "a flavor of the month". They continue to channel their seemingly unwanted energy into negative outlets, leeching the curiosity and positivity of peers. And finally, to be generous, let us consider one-half of the remaining 70% on the fence will adopt the new system. This results in 50% engaged staff. Not bad, but not enough for critical mass.

Now reflect on the Lean Empowerment System. The engaged staff (15%) can be assumed, but they are not static. These are the Lateral Leaders who rotate every 1.5 years to allow others the chance to participate in the process of change. After one rotation, another 15% from the 70% on the fence are pulled into the culture of change and convinced of its merit from the inside. If we assume half of the staff on the fence adopt the new system (35%), 15% are engaged in year one, another 15% rotate in year two, we are already left with 50% of folks on the fence, and 15% engaged, resulting in

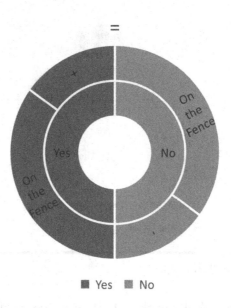

Figure 6.2 Engaged staff in a lean production system.

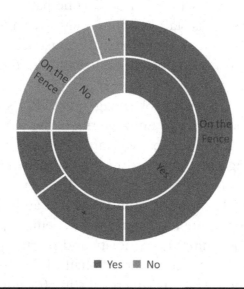

Figure 6.3 Engaged staff in a lean empowerment system.

65% engagement. And this doesn't even factor in the most important group: detractors. The detractors are split between 10% complainers and 5% "culture casualties" who eventually leave and look elsewhere for an employer to accommodate their denial.[29] The remaining complainers, our change agents in hiding, become the greatest asset to the company. Leaders covet their candor and invest in their unwillingness to settle. This brings us to 75% engagement (Figure 6.3): more than enough to create sustainable momentum. And, as one study shows, the doubling of engagement from 30% of staff to 60% would result in +12% production, −27% turnover, and −40% safety events.[30]

But change isn't *that* simple. We cannot expect people to flock to a new suggestion system. We must continue to explore human behavior in the face of change. It is not uncommon for most ideas to come from the minority of staff. The limitation is not fear, but disillusionment. Staff are jaded that nobody will do anything with the ideas. And recent studies compiled by Harvard Business Review reinforce this point: the biggest reason for withholding ideas and concerns isn't fear. It is the belief that managers won't do anything about them.[31]

So far, we have argued that a suggestion system is not merely a list of inputs and outputs. It is, at its core, an Empowerment System. Each idea, according to Imai, is "a sign workers have more skill than their job calls for."[32] It is symbolic of so much more untapped energy that is waiting to be channeled into simplifying processes for the benefit of everyone. And the absence of ideas is not the ultimate concern of an Empowerment System, like it is for the Production System: "Sometimes it is the lack of new ideas that inhibits improvement, but more often it's employees inability to break out of unproductive work habits that limits change."[33] It all comes back to the people, their virtues, and their vices.

We will pick back up on this thread in the following section on Standard Work, but first, let me pause to call attention to an important matter.

A Warning: Motivation and Rewards

I must offer a warning to wrap up our analysis of the suggestion system. Leaders must resist the temptation to bribe staff into submitting ideas. We cannot buy ideas, just like we cannot buy Lateral Leaders. Coercion takes many forms, from explicit financial payouts to "friendly" interdepartmental competitions. The gamification of work seems harmless. And it is our first instinct. But we must pause to understand how it *really* impacts staff.

In a Production System, the currency of engagement is the volume of ideas submitted by staff. For example, Toyota employees submit 1.5 million suggestions per year.[34] They strive to maximize their "learn to burn ratio," which can "generate the maximum insight from each dollar spent."[35] As a result, the role of management is judged based on how many ideas are submitted by staff.[36] Under this new pressure, systems will inevitably start to incentivize behavior that draws ideas out of staff no matter the consequences. Many contemporary books on Lean Production detail some of the most popular ways to elicit ideas from staff. These vary based on organization but include models of payment for the most impactful ideas, contests, or competitions. But, according to extensive research conducted by Alfie Kohn, rewards and punishment are equally ineffective – they are both attempts of leadership to influence human behavior toward a desired outcome. The carrot and the stick are no different; both are used to control. And both are based on a warped understanding of human motivation.

Kohn argues how "it is most important to avoid rewarding people for engaging in an activity or behavior that we would *like* them to find intrinsically motivating."[37] If it is already something not interesting, adding rewards does not help.[38] He goes on to break down numerous assumptions we hold to be true. For example, it is easy to believe how "the more credit we give the more ideas we get."[39] But Kohn quotes a study about people who are offered rewards and how they "choose easier tasks, are less efficient… and tend to be answer oriented and more illogical in their problem-solving strategies."[40] This is the opposite goal of Kaizen. He also challenges the use of contests, which are successful in the short term but detrimental for the long term. Contests lead to "a diminished sense of empowerment and less responsibility for their future performance."[41] People learn to play to the rules of the contest instead of basing their work on an intrinsic motivation to succeed. Either the system sets the goals too low, which wastes human potential. Or staff come to recognize the systematic problems beyond their control and become disengaged in future changes.

Instead of motivating through rewards or punishment, Kohn proposes 3Cs that we must integrate into a system during its design: Collaborative, Content, Choice.[42] Leaders must avoid the temptation to control with a carrot or a stick and instead create collaborative environments for staff to work together, challenge what content is truly valuable, and release ownership (choice) over the decision-making process. And, although it may seem somewhat counterintuitive, this comes about through Standards. In an Empowerment System, standardization exists to provide clarity. It gives staff something to use their voice to change. Standard Work is the unlikely basis of empowerment.

Standard Work

A standard is an element of a system and not an end (telos) in itself. In a Lean Production System, standard work is a prerequisite for improvement and assumes that improvement will follow.[43] According to *Standard Work for Lean Healthcare*, "Standardization is not only adherence to standards but also the continual creation of new and better standards."[44] The simple presence of a standard helps us identify variation since there is an anchor from which staff can observe drifting. It is both scientific and experimental, a hypothesis or theory that must be challenged. Our goal is to identify problems and eventually find a better way.[45]

Standard work in a Lean Empowerment System is a target that staff can collectively point at and channel improvement energy into. It may seem counterintuitive, but the goal of a standard is not standardization. It is empowerment, with standardization and improvement as a result. The creation of the first standard, a hypothesis at best, is an empowering process for the Lateral Leaders and the entire Process Improvement Team. Frontline staff are given the opportunity to participate in a process that is otherwise reserved for a centralized training team. Then the standard is posted and becomes an open-source code into which staff can channel frustration, leverage for peer education, or point to for confidence. The managers, who were previously responsible for the outcomes of staff, can now free themselves from the administrative burden of knowing the daily intricacies of each role and confidently focus energy into areas with compounding returns like strategy or mentorship. And, as a result, the frontline staff follow the standard, less out of a forced mechanical adherence, and more out of ownership and trust.

Our core understanding of Standard Work must change from a top-down edict to a peer-to-peer (Chapter 5) open-source code (Chapter 4). Imagine a football team where the players co-create the playbook with the coaching staff and participate in the play-calling. We sometimes see this among veteran quarterbacks, regarded as experts among their peers, who participate in play-calling from the field. The microphone in his helmet is a direct line to the coach, and he may wear a cuff with the plays listed as a reference. He may even call an audible without asking the coaches' permission based on what he sees in the defense. We must continue to encourage this type of peer-lead decision-making to redefine everything we know about standards in the workplace. Because the word "standard" carries baggage from Management Dependence and Urgency Dependence, two of the Vices of Production. It insinuates control. And it is just shy of being a policy or regulation, the ultimate administrative red tape. The Lean Empowerment System must reclaim the idea of Standard Work for it to be useful once again.

The rest of this chapter is a composition of ideas on Standard Work from both primary sources and secondary sources redirected around the goals of an Empowerment System. We will first discuss the problem of variation that standardization aims to tackle. Then we will address opposing views on when to write a standard (before or after improvement). The standardization process will be broken up into two sections: How to write standard work (SDCA), and how to improve standard work (PDCA). Finally, we will peel away the layers of standard work for leaders and gain a fresh perspective on a topic that is rarely addressed: Standards must differ for frontline staff and leaders, an idea that most contemporary literature overlooks.

The Problem: Variation

Variation evokes a gut reaction. Although we may not have the words to describe it, we know it when we see it.

Recall virtue theory from Chapter 1. Variation manifests as excess or deficiency in virtue theory. The golden mean is a range of control, where each person has boundaries in which they can remain virtuous without crossing a line into vice. Similarly, in the framework of statistical control theory, variation is any point outside the defined control limits of a process. This is where we get the phrase "out of control." These two theories, virtue and statistical control, share a lot in common. And they teach us about the problem that standard work seeks to address.

The study of statistical control theory was first introduced by Walter Shewhart in the early 1900s. He argued that human activity tends to exist in a state of chaos in the absence of control. A zone of control is defined once there are enough similar data points or recurring actions to predict future outcomes. An average is measured from a set of data and mathematical formulas determine how many "sigmas," or standard deviations, from the average are allowed in each direction. Data points are deemed "out of control" or "unwanted variability" if they meet certain criteria, such as one or more data points falling outside the control limits, seven consecutive data points increasing or decreasing, or eight consecutive data points on one side of the average.[46] This variation, also defined by Kahneman as system "noise," is "inconsistency, and inconsistency damages the credibility of the system."[47] Statistical control is about retaining the creditability for staff and creating predictability for leadership. And process improvements attempt to move the state of statistical control to an improved average and build trust in a system.

The balance between Kai ("change") and Zen ("right state") brings a system to a new state of statistical control. Only after the right state is reached can it aspire to a new and better right state.

There is a caveat to variation: not all variation is unwanted. All living things rely on it for survival. According to Geoffrey West's book, *Scale*, variation among people "is just the first step in evolution." At a biological level, "genetic variance is generated by mutation (random point changes in the DNA code) and recombination (rearrangements of fragments of DNA)."[48] It is part of nature.

Each one of us experiences variation on a smaller scale in the workplace. Many of our ideas for improvement come from the variations that naturally arise in the different contexts between offices or departments. New hires may bring variant ideas from their past employers that can expose problems in the current system. A workaround may become the standard. Or an unlikely combination of inputs results in an innovative output. In any case, since variation will exist, we must ask: "what does it tell us about the process and the people?"[49] Some "accidents" may be truly detrimental, whereas others are, in the words of painter Bob Ross, "happy accidents." Variation may lead to errors or breakthroughs. It is up to the system to provide the right guardrails to drive variation in a productive direction.

As we have seen, a great deal of nuance is required when we discuss variation and standards. Some variations lead to extinction, and others, survival. Some systems eradicate variants, whereas others encourage them. And, even still, some people consider control, the opposite of variation, as overly structured or stifling. Each one of us has experienced "impersonal rules"[50] in the name of stability. But no matter the situation, it is critical that we frequently discuss the effects of variation, standards, and control charts in an Empowerment System. These tools are meant to build trust, create predictability, and monitor improvement, not hold over the heads of staff.

Juran encourages us to "challenge the standard as much as the variance."[51] Let us now pivot from the problem, variation, to the solution, standardization.

The Solution: Standardization

We are immediately faced with a difficult "chicken or the egg" scenario: do we improve first, and then standardize, or standardize first, and then improve? Let us consider the benefits and shortcomings of each.

Option 1 – Improve, then Standardize:

This order is common in A3s, PDCAs, and Six Sigma projects that rely on Value Stream Analysis or Process Mapping exercises. The book *Standard Work for the Shopfloor* argues that standard work is the "final stage of implementing lean production."[52] Leaders often choose improvement before standardization if they want to show movement and experience quick wins. They place a great deal of focus on improvement, which consequently leaves little energy or attention for the standard work. A project team may lose focus or enthusiasm for a project by the time when it matters most. This approach is dependent on management, projects, and urgency, three of the vices of production.

Option 2 – Standardize, then Improve:

The book *Standard Work for Lean Healthcare* argues that we must instead "begin at the end."[53] Although he recognizes that Lean practitioners tend to standardize at the end of PDCA, he recommends flipping the process. Recall the two pillars of Lean introduced on the first page of this book: Continuous Improvement and Respect for People. If inconsistency harms the credibility of a system, and standards build trust, then *our ability to respect people is threatened by the absence of standards.*[54] According to *Shingo Principles*, "Great leaders never let their teams work without a standard. It is not just poor management; it is disrespectful."[55] The drive for continuous improvement must remain secondary to respect for people.

An overlooked idea from Masaaki Imai is the key to unlocking a new way of improvement. First, we must *SDCA* (Standardize, Do, Check, Act), then *PDCA* (Plan, Do, Check, Act).[56] The act of PDCA raises the standard created in the first SDCA, "only after a standard has been established."[57] According to Deming, in his quote from a lecture by Juran, "Removing all special causes is one step toward improvement and brings the system back to where it should have always been."[58] Our journey to improvement doesn't begin until a process is in control. We must balance SDCA with PDCA, just as we balance the two seasons of Juran (control and breakthrough) and Imai (improvement and maintenance). Even Intermountain Health, a potent force in the world of Lean, employs a model that is similar to SDCA to generate learning: "standardize, implement, override, modify."[59] It is critical to recognize that "Kaizen on top of chaos will only equal more chaos."[60] Any PDCA model that fails to start with SDCA or pause for SDCA after an improvement is at risk of injecting chaotic energy into an unstable system.

We can point at two reasons, both rooted in human nature, that explain why a system avoids SDCA and jumps straight into PDCA.

1. First, the process of writing standards is *boring*. Very few people wake up in the morning with the innate longing to write standards. Nobody says, "I can't wait to write a standard today!" But, according to *Standard Work for the Shopfloor*, although "it seems boring," it actually "leads to increases in creativity, improvement, and job satisfaction."[61]
2. Second, choosing SDCA means taking a hard look in the mirror and *accepting reality*. What we see might be ugly, but we can only fix a process after we bask in its broken glory. Although our first instinct is to avoid broken things, we must try to use the brokenness as a tool for change. According to Taiichi Ohno (142), a team should "document exactly what you are doing now. If you make it better than now, it is *kaizen*. If not, and you establish the best possible way, the motivation for *kaizen* will be gone. That is why one way of motivating people to do *kaizen* is to create a poor standard." The broken glory of SDCA will naturally spark PDCA.

Recall how virtue is the balance between absence and excess. In the absence of standards, the PDCA cycle will arise to fill the space. This is the most common outcome. Or, in excess, standardization can smother the spark of PDCA and hide problems. According to *Noise*, "Rules will simply drive discretion underground."[62]

Those who set a standard (SDCA) before improving (PDCA) must follow an important rule to avoid this vice of excess: It must do more good than bad. Consider a traffic stoplight: red lights waste time and cause a delay for drivers. But they reduce accidents at intersections. City planners must justify if the delay, in the words of Deming, "offers more advantage than the economic waste that it entails."[63] Any rule must be "reasonable, prudent, and feasible."[64] According to systems theory, the best way to avoid excessive standardization is to set minimum specifications or requirements, then "get out of the way."[65] Set a standard, then let human nature run its course.

But Wait… Don't Standards Threaten My Freedom?

Quite the opposite, actually.

Think of the last time you said, "I am so busy," or heard "busy" as a response to the question "How are you?" Most of us do it without noticing because busyness is a badge of pride that tells people "Look how important I am!" It associates capacity with value. The more work I am doing, or others *perceive* I am doing, the more valuable I am to the organization. We tend to self-induce chaos to feel productive.

The momentary comfort of perceived busyness masks the reality of our broken glory. It is a band aid that provides momentary relief from a festering wound of inefficiency. These underlying inefficiencies do not see the light of day if we are afraid to confront them. And some virtue theorists go as far to claim that busyness has even become the new sloth. Laziness (deficiency) has been replaced by busyness (excess) or the façade of busyness. The common business idea, "look like you are working," is the ultimate waste of human potential. It is both vice and self-deception.

Standard Work sets us free from self-imposed chaos. The opposite of chaos, Zen (right state), replaces busyness and gives us the foundation for kai (change). Only after we accept standardization as a prerequisite for freedom can true innovation exist. This is repeated throughout both historical and contemporary Lean literature:

- The removal of non-creative tasks will make room for creativity.[66]
- Standardization frees us from menial tasks to focus on important tasks.[67]
- Turn complex intuition (intuitive medicine) into repeatable tasks (empirical medicine).[68]
- "By stabilizing part of the care, we create more room for good thinking" and create "capacity for the truly unique."[69]
- "Statistical control opened the way to engineering innovation. Without statistical control, the process was in unstable chaos, the noise of which would mask the effect of any attempt to bring improvement. With statistical control achieved, engineers and chemists became innovative, creative. They now had an identifiable process."[70]

This recurring idea is well summarized in the book *Atomic Habits*: "Habits don't restrict freedom – they create it."[71] The wardrobe of the 44th President of the United States is a great example of this. During his time in office, Barack Obama only owned two types of suits. He concluded that his energy should not be wasted on menial decisions and instead channeled into decisions that mattered.[72] Standardization set him free from inconsequential choices and made room for creativity. And it can do the same for each of us, even if we are not the President.

How to Write Standard Work (SDCA)

It is important that we gain insight into the process of writing Standard Work (SDCA) before trying to improve Standard Work (PDCA). There are a few tools that can help us learn about this foundational process. Each one can teach us a lesson.

The Float and the 80/20 Rule

Lesson: A standard should align with 80% of staff in a role, not the 20%.

The 80/20 Rule is based on the Pareto Principle, which theorizes how 80% of outcomes come from 20% of the causes. Process Improvement Teams employ the 80/20 Rule in statistical analysis to identify which causes to address first. Now we must broaden our understanding and application of the 80/20 Rule for the sake of creating Standard Work in a Lean Empowerment System.

It is common for organizations to employ teams of centrally managed floats that can step in when a department is short-staffed due to illness, time off, or training. The floats often hear the phrases "we do things a little different here" or "I'm not sure that will work here" as a defense of variation. For one reason or another, local teams justify breaking away from the standard in favor of a process that serves their needs. They may be a few steps ahead of the curve, hiding their discoveries from other similar departments, or they may be years behind. I quickly compared this response to the grumblings I hear among staff when a new standard is launched. Some staff go as far to exclaim, "We are all different!"

I frequently share a mantra with teams who are attempting to write standard work for the first time: *Write a standard with the float in mind.* Floats cannot hide behind a local culture. They are not privy to the excuses listed above. Each day they float to a new process and do not have time for anything but the standard. In the absence of standard work or Lateral Leaders, the float is the closest thing you have to a system. They embody the 80% that is the same between staff and are immersed daily in the 20% that differs based on the department.

So why do people focus so much on the 20%?

First, the 20% is flashy and makes a good story. For example, after the birth of my first child, my eyes were opened to the world of diapers and the inexplicable messes she could make at her petite size. I remember retelling a story a dozen or more times about a blowout my daughter had as my wife and I were trying to leave a restaurant. It was five minutes past close, and the staff were giving us a mixture of looks, from complete disgust to total understanding (the latter coming from who I could assume are also parents) as I sprinted across the room holding my daughter in the air like Simba as I looked for the nearest restroom. Her clothing was beyond saving, and it ended up in the trash with what could no longer be identified as a diaper. Half-naked baby in one hand, and disheveled diaper bag in the other, I proudly marched back to our table, increased the amount I left as a tip, and proceeded to my car. The funny thing is this single blowout not only represented the 20%, but probably the 0.002% of the many and, thankfully, less exciting diaper changes I have made in my time as a dad. But my friends and co-workers would much rather hear this story than a dull recounting of a basic diaper change.

The 20% is also a distracting scapegoat. It leeches energy and creativity away from the core processes. Only after the 80% is defined can the 20% warrant a discussion. Consider this example: a healthcare organization opened a public vaccine clinic to serve hundreds of patients each day. Children were not allowed in the clinic for safety reasons. During an end-of-day debrief, the team voiced "this would all go smoothly if the kids weren't here!" and spent the next twenty minutes planning how to deal with children the next day. As the meeting ended, other operational questions remained unanswered. But they had a plan for addressing the presence of kids in the clinic! After the debrief, and upon further questioning, the team discovered that only two children were in the clinic all day, comprising less than 1% of total patients seen. Everyone was left wondering if the unanswered questions would have made a bigger impact.

We see this in almost every profession. Businesses must invest first in the infrastructure of their flagship products. Athletes must practice the foundations before applying advanced techniques. Artists must study and replicate the greats before making a name for themselves. These examples, and many others, repeat the same message: We cannot dream of being innovative until we are proficient. Our limited resource of time must be focused on improving the 80% first. And staff can only start to differentiate between innovative variation and entropic variation after the 80% is accepted as the standard. Until then, they hide side by side in one large pool of variation.

Organizations miss out on a valuable rhetorical tool if we limit the 80/20 Rule to mere statistical analysis. This tool can save frontline staff, Lateral Leaders, and the Process Improvement Team a lot of time and energy going down rabbit-holes that don't apply to most people. Asking, "is this part of the 80 or the 20?" is the least disrespectful way to "parking lot" an idea and stay focused on the standard. Teams are quick to understand this natural guardrail, even starting ideas with "I know I'm probably the 20% here…" And, once systems are in place to address the 80%, local teams can start to address the 20% of local variations that make us truly unique.

The "Middle Flow"

Lesson: Standardize task-based roles before intuition-based roles.

Each role will respond differently to standards. Therefore, it matters which type of staff are standardized first. An organization is wise to standardize task-based roles before the roles that demand high levels of intuition. For example, the business roles in medicine (registration, scheduling, management, etc.) must come before the clinical roles (medical assistants, nurses, care managers, advanced practice providers, physicians, etc.). Staff in business roles tend to be more flexible and forgiving as administrators test new things. Clinical staff are less willing to experiment, viewing their work as a tension between rigid standards set by national or state levels, and an art that differs from patient to patient.

We can translate this tension into a doctor's visit. Toussaint explains how we cannot start by standardizing the "middle flow," the part of the visit where the provider meets with the patient. Even a whisper about standardizing this process will unsettle providers.[73] Instead, we must first focus on the "upstream flow", which is everything before the patient enters the exam room, and the "downstream flow," everything after she exits the exam room. These two flows tend to touch more business roles than clinical roles.

This rule also applies when applying standards to patient care. Many processes inaccurately place the patient at the center when the next customer is another staff member. An organization, in the words of Toussaint, must "work on solving physician and staff problems first, before attacking more patient-focused issues. This may sound like backward priorities, but this is the way that you will win over the people who will then use lean-repeatedly to improve patient experiences."[74]

Habits, Error-Proofing, and Choice Architecture

Lesson: A standard should be the only way, or at least the easiest way, to do a task.

The way that we design a standard will determine the likelihood it is followed. Let us first understand habit and discipline as key components of human nature. Then, we will explore two ways to make a standard stick: error proofing and choice architecture.

Habit: Standard work lives in the realm of habit formation. According to Markovitz, "Habits are standard work that become reflexive."[75] Psychologists have argued back and forth for decades over the exact number of times we must do an action for it to become habitual. Despite disagreements on the exact answer, we know that the formation of a habit takes time and effort. Negative habits are easy to form, and healthy habits take effort. Habits are the "compound interest of self-improvement," resulting in virtuous or vicious cycles.[76] We commonly hear the idea of compound interest applied to finances, especially retirement savings. Let it sit, and it will grow. Dip in, and it may actively deplete. Both are habits that we can form and control.

But our culture prefers instant gratification to the gradual formation of habits. Diets, for example, use a vice – excess or deficiency – to retrain the human body toward a certain end. Some weightlifters eat in excess to achieve bulking, and many more practice deficiency to lose weight. As a result, our bodies adapt to the new normal and start to require specific nutrients to stay in a state of control. But after the diet, weight gain or weight loss is inevitable, and even increases, when the dieter reintroduces elements from their previous lifestyle. The human body and habit cannot be cheated.

But wait! What if I told you there was a way to achieve perfect self-control over our habits *without* a fad diet or magic pill? The answer is system design. For example, if you are tempted to eat candy in your house, then do not bring candy into your house. If you spend too much time on your phone in bed, then charge your phone in the living room. The examples are as numerous as the choices we make. And it is easier to set these types of limits in a system than fight our human nature with discipline and habits. We must design our life in a way that does not require self-control.[77]

To consistently achieve the desired outcome from a process, we must make the best way the only way, or at least the easiest way. And if the best choice is not the easiest choice, our human nature will favor the path of least resistance. According to Hines and Butterworth, "Keep the habits as simple as possible. It is very easy to make things complicated."[78] Complicated standards are less likely to be followed or elicit feedback.

Error-Proofing: Shingeo Shingo introduced a now popular idea to the Lean Production System called Poka-Yoke, translated as error proofing. Error proofing builds quality control into each step of the process and handoff between workers instead of relying on quality control specialists at the final step of production. It level-loads the accountability for quality across the entire team, reducing the waste of inspection and valuing the work of each person along the way. According to Deming, the process of inspection is "equivalent to planning for defects."[79] Like Poka-Yoke, a standard must attempt to reduce the possibility of errors through habit and automation.

One example of habitual error proofing is 5S, a popular process that gives every item, habit, or process a home.[80] The 5 Ss are Sort, Set in Order, Shine, Standardize, Sustain. Take for example this story: I shave every morning using a basic manual razor that is stored in my bathroom drawer. One day, I reached into the drawer of jostled items and cut my hand on the razor hidden among other items. Committed to avoiding another painful cut, I emptied the drawer to evaluate what I needed and what could be discarded. I separated items into daily use (razor, facial towel, deodorant, mouthguard) and infrequent use (contact prescriptions, electric razor, nail clippers) and purchased bins for each category. I thought my 5S was complete, but I still risked injury as I reached for my exposed razor. Until one day I opened the drawer and noticed that my wife had cleaned the laundry and laid a fresh facial towel on top of the razor. I was able to use the towel to pick up the razor and then wrapped it in the towel as I put it away. I haven't cut my hand since adding this simple step. My morning routine is now error proofed.

Choice Architecture: Choice architecture is a tool from process engineering that makes the best way the *easiest way*. We often use this tool when it is impossible to make the best way the *only way*. This is also known as a default, making the best way the most basic way.[81] Consider the Dash Button launched by Amazon in 2015 for the simple repurchasing of household items. A small button with a brand logo can be stuck anywhere in your home and is synced up with your Amazon account. You simply push the button when you notice you are getting low, and the item will appear at your doorstep. Amazon encourages consumers to purchase Dash Buttons for any common household item that you purchase on a frequent basis. It is easy for you and makes easy money for them.

A few years later, Amazon launched a new product called the Dash Smart Shelf to pair with Dash Buttons. Amazon wanted to make it *even easier* for consumers to unconsciously reorder items in the most efficient manner. First, the user places a full supply of an item on the shelf and logs the weight of each item in the system. An order is automatically placed when the weight drops below a set point, known as the par level.

Zero intervention is required, and both Amazon and the consumer get what they want.

The Dash Button is an example of error-proofing, and the Dash Smart Shelf is an example of choice architecture. Both are preferable to the lone formation of a habit, which relies on our forgetful and easily tempted human nature. And as we have seen, error-proofing and choice architecture are two methods for understanding the interplay between habit and standard work. It is up to leadership, those with the hand on the wheel, to learn and recognize the patterns, habits, and traditions that support virtuous cycles and then position them above vicious cycles.[82]

National Standards Are Starting Points

Lesson: National standards are a starting point for quality, not the end point.

The healthcare space is bursting with policies, procedures, and measures for success. According to the Group Practice Journal, a monthly publication about Medical Groups, "CMS [Centers for Medicare and Medicaid Services] has approximately 1700 measures for providers within different practice settings. Combine that with over 80 Healthcare Effectiveness Data and Information Set (HEDIS) along with 57 Measures the Joint Commission uses."[83] Individual insurance plans also have their own goals. Organizations set internal benchmarks. And we haven't even mentioned the most confusing part: sometimes the definitions or criteria for success differ between sources, like the Hemoglobin A1c score for high-risk Diabetics.

It is important to assume, out of positive intent, that a national standard exists because an organization should consider it as important. It is therefore the responsibility of healthcare organizations to use all these metrics as a starting point, not the end point, on their journey to quality. According to Kohn, we need to evaluate *what* we are encouraging when we motivate with national standards.[84] The first question a system must ask is "is this really worth doing?"

Ishikawa and Deming echo these concerns and express strong opinions about our reliance on mandatory regulations and national standards to drive up quality. Ishikawa states, "I have been advocating the position that 'quality control cannot be implemented by merely following national or international standards. These standards may be taken into consideration, but beyond these standards quality control must have the higher goals of meeting the requirements of consumers and creating quality which satisfies them.'"[85]

He continues, "the mere fact of meeting national standards or specifications is not the answer. It is simply insufficient."[86] Deming echoes this sentiment and focuses on the interplay between national and local standards. He argues that an organization must "avoid the useless proliferation of mandatory regulations to fill the gap left by a lack of voluntary standards."[87] Both of them leave us with food for thought to take back into our own organizations. We must constantly analyze and evaluate the standards around us.

Beware the Binder

Lesson: A standard should be digital, written by frontline staff, and explain "why."

There are two types of education: orientation and ongoing. It is important for the standard to be the source of truth for both.[88] I often hear staff express how "a standard would be helpful for new hires but not for experienced staff." Assumptions like this are remnants of the Lean Production System and a defense mechanism used by veteran team members to avoid the possibility of change. The same staff will likely refer to a binder in their file cabinet they received during orientation as their source of truth. They hold tight to this tome as their first comfort blanket, a bible of content that will forever remain relevant in their eyes. As a result, staff struggle to view the orientation manual as something that can be improved or changed. It either binds the user to an outdated process or gathers dust.

The conversion of training materials into standard work is the first step of the improvement process. But beware of what you might find. Digital resources may hardly get used. Entire teams may devote their time to tools that are left untouched. Weekly or monthly newsletters may sit unread in inboxes. The sheer volume of new releases, process changes, and tip sheets may overwhelm the very people they are designed to help. No wonder staff create their own personal standards; if there is not a single source of truth that is easy to use, the standard will never become a habit.

Organizations often rely on a centralized education team for the creation of training documents. These documents are the closest thing to a standard in the absence of intentional Standard Work. It is a good start, emphasizing what is taught in orientation, but it fails to address ongoing education. Lean Empowerment Systems must shift the focus of education from an orientation-heavy approach to ongoing education.

An orientation-heavy approach is easy to manage since it can rely on minimal inputs. Leadership can set the GPS coordinates and use the same training for years. Changes are only made when completely necessary. But ongoing education assumes the presence of change and relies on the input of frontline staff. And it is messy. Now, assume general orientation happens every other week. A small change to orientation could mean one group will have a different training from the class two weeks later. Someone must be responsible for training the staff from the first training to ensure the standard is maintained. Leadership and the frontline must carefully discern the best way to orient and provide ongoing education while respecting people and encouraging continuous improvement. It is no easy task, but it is necessary.

Thankfully, the Lateral Leader can reduce administrative headaches by helping bridge the gap between orientation and ongoing education. Frontline staff tend to be more willing than leaders to treat a standard process as the current best way of doing a job, not a policy set in stone. They understand that change is a defining value of standard work. Also, staff will not self-inflict the suffocation of countless tip sheets on their peers or themselves. They are fully aware of the cacophony of distractions that already pull them away from daily tasks. Anything worthwhile must be malleable, succinct, and easy to access.

Finally, standards must connect the "How" with the "Why" of each task.[89] Leadership, technical teams, and Lateral Leaders must collaborate to meet this challenge head-on, or they risk the mechanical language that Complex Adaptive Systems (CAS) worked so hard to reverse. The Lateral Leader must describe the local context and catalog the internal forces that influence frontline staff, while leadership explains the external forces that make a task so important. The technical teams must balance the "ideal" way with the realistic current state of her local employer. It is critical that each team remember they work in service to the frontline staff, not the bottom line or another force.

It is valuable to summarize our lessons learned from SDCA before moving on.

- A standard should align with 80% of staff in a role, not the 20%.
- Standardize task-based roles before intuition-based roles.
- A standard should be the only way, or at least the easiest way, to do a task.
- National standards are a starting point for quality, not the end point.
- A standard should be digital, written by frontline staff, and explain "why."

We can transition from the process of writing a standard (SDCA) into improvement (PDCA) once the standard is posted in a shared space. Standardization is a critical step, but it doesn't last long. The longer a standard spends in SDCA, the more likely a system suffers from chronic complacency. Let us now turn our attention to the improvement process.

How to Improve Standard Work (PDCA)

Constructive Complaining

A core tenet of process improvement is the correct identification of a problem before proposing a solution. Recall the quote from Charles Kettering: "A problem well stated is a problem half-solved." Popular Lean tools like Value Stream Mapping, Root Cause Analysis, and Ishikawa Diagrams start with a problem and meticulously dissect the causes to find a reasonable change. Healthcare workers, like process engineers, are wary of solutions that address the symptoms instead of the cause. These will not make a sustainable impact on the health of the person. Instead, we must embrace a wholly different source of ideas, and a staple of lateral thinking: *complaints*. Just as complaints help a clinician diagnose a patient's condition, a complaint can help a process engineer discover waste while respecting the complainer.

Henry Ford famously said, "Don't find fault, find a remedy; anybody can complain."[90] This idea makes sense at face value but is contrary to both the Lean Production System and Empowerment System. The problem with encouraging solutions to problems is twofold: we might overlook the real problem as we jump to conclusions (Lean Production), and we miss the chance to empower staff along the way (Lean Empowerment). And according to Clark, "sometimes [staff] don't know how or have the confidence" to submit solutions, but they have the confidence to complain.[91] We must challenge the long-standing philosophy of Ford and create a culture that encourages constructive complaints.

It is the shared responsibility of leaders and staff in an Empowerment System to "lower what is usually a too-high bar for what's considered appropriate conversation."[92] Leaders must create an atmosphere that allows complaints instead of solutions. The common "suggestion system" should be redefined as a "complaint system," since "'suggestion' implies you have to submit and gain permission before implementing an idea."[93] This will consequently increase retention and lead to stronger performance.[94]

Juran urges us to "establish an atmosphere that permits a free flow of open-ended, supplemental questions."[95] And if we want to create this atmosphere we must also understand the two reasons why people don't complain and stay silent instead: Fear of being viewed negatively by peers, and fear of damaging work relationships.[96] Both are rooted in relationship, the currency of the Empowerment System.

It is easy for leaders to convert a complaint into an idea. Simply change the period to a question mark and add "Why" at the beginning of the sentence. "It really bugs me when my knee hurts after running three miles" is converted into "Why does my knee hurt after three miles?" "The number of clicks to scan in a document is annoying" is converted into "Why are there so many clicks to scan in a document?" Leaders who apply this algorithm will become masters of reframing. We must prune, train, and harvest the complaints as soon as they are ripe enough to prepare. Otherwise, we will wait months for a single idea if we limit suggestions to solutions instead of just ideas.

Staff must also follow a simple ground rule about complaining: "be hard on the process, not on the people." The presence of Standard Work gives both leaders and frontline staff a non-human target toward which they can channel their energy. Masaaki Imai defines a problem as a step in the process that inconveniences another person upstream or downstream, but not the person who causes it.[97] Labeling someone as the problem is not a helpful complaint. In a way, it jumps to the conclusion that the person is the fault in the system, not their action. It distracts from the problems in the system or the process that caused the problems and instead relies on an *ad hominem* argument that challenges the very existence of another person. Thomas Graham explains this distinction in a similar way, as *criticism* and *critical analysis*: "Pure criticism diminishes all parties, while critical analysis is a requirement of the innovator leader, because it identifies shortcomings and paves the way for improvement."[98] The words we use have power; for example, is less insulting to call someone a "person experiencing homelessness" instead of "homeless." The former description can help us ask "what is causing your homelessness?" to challenge the system that caused the experience of homelessness. This question is more useful than asking "why are you homeless?," a value statement which assumes the person is the cause of their own homelessness.

The use of language can also reduce ambiguity in a system and give staff permission to complain, another form of cover in exchange for candor. Many leaders have found it helpful to explicitly "assign dissent" as a means of giving staff permission to complain.[99] Software design firms hire "white hackers" to purposefully hack their code to find flaws or gaps. Similarly, we give people permission to dissent when they preface their statement with "let me play devil's advocate." It is also common between staff and a consumer. Organizations will elicit dissent from consumers with an important goal in mind: to convert potential complaints into active complaints. In the words of Ishikawa, "We ask consumers not to be docile and to say what must be said as a means of helping manufacturers create better quality products...Companies must encourage consumers to complain."[100] It is clear how innovation at any level requires constructive dissent.[101]

The opposite of dissent is silence, an omen in Lean Empowerment.[102] Complaining, in contrast, is good for us.[103] And its absence is a sign that we have denied our human nature and succumbed to complacency. Consider the junk drawer that is commonplace in the American kitchen. It is the home to half-used gift cards, rubber bands, sticky notes, dead batteries, pens, and expired coupons, to name a few items. Now, imagine if we locked the drawer open for an entire week and you had to stare into the black hole every time you walked by. Would the drawer be the same by the end of the week? Likely not. This is because complacency is a learned experience. Our natural tendency is to reduce chaos and remove waste. But our sensitivity to waste is dulled over time. To encourage complaining means "rebuilding a team's sensitivity to waste and encourage behavior that is not complacent."[104]

A system's comfort level with complaints is directly correlative to its success with empowerment. This is of utmost importance because complaints are a symbol of trust in the Empowerment System. They are proof that staff are willing to identify problems and voice them in a raw and unfiltered manner. Silence, in contrast, should never be assumed as consent. Rather, it means that staff are uncomfortable with speaking up. The absence of complaints is the most troubling sign for an organization that seeks a culture of true empowerment.

Silence from leadership is equally detrimental as silence among staff. It is critical that every complaint or idea elicits a response from the Lateral Leaders, even if the idea is not possible. In surveys of more than 3,500 employees in multiple companies, a study from Detert and Burris published in Harvard Business Review found that "bosses' failure to close the loop increased subordinates' belief that speaking up was futile by 30%. But if managers had closed the loop in the past, their reports spoke up 19% more frequently."[105] A simple response, even an undesired one, goes a long way. No response to a suggestion is "worse than outright rejection – which is at least an acknowledgment."[106]

The primary goal of improvement in the Lean Empowerment System is to increase respect for people. Respect correlates with increases in pride of work. Deming, in *Out of the Crisis*, explains: "The aim of leadership should be to improve the performance of man and machine, to improve quality, to increase output, and simultaneously to bring pride of workmanship to people."[107] Sherkenbach further draws out this idea in his commentary on Deming: "I am often asked, 'How can we leapfrog our competition in the international market place?' I think the answer lies in the ability to promote, in our *formal processes*, the ability to find joy in our work."[108] Joy is difficult to attain if staff are not allowed to systemically relieve themselves from the burden of complaints. Ideas, as we have explored in this section, often start as complaints. This natural human tendency, when restricted, will lead to a buildup of resentment and complacency that stifles pride of work and suffocates human potential. Leaders must learn to silence their base fear of complaints. Each complaint has a raw power waiting to be tapped.

The Role of Managers When Standards Exist

The feedback loop between frontline staff and the Process Improvement Team does not include the local manager. It is an independent yet complementary process that is meant to extend a pressure relief valve to the manager, freeing up their time for the work of local empowerment. The manager gains a canned response to ideas or complaints: "Have you submitted that to your Process Improvement Team?" or "Have you asked your Lateral Leaders?" The ability to defer issues to peers will come naturally to some managers, either out of desperation or true empowerment. But for others it will feel like a tooth extraction. The local managers who are resistant tend to attach their meaning or purpose to solving the problems of their direct reports. Deferring to a system means losing their definition of self. We must realize how this twofold vice of hero and management dependence is really holding managers back. And we must hang up the firefighting hat and don the mantle of transformation.

A manager is a partner on the journey to empowerment. According to Batalden, a prominent voice in the field of microsystems theory, "It is tempting to think of leading as what a person—the leader—does. But what if you consider the three commonly used words leader, leadership, and leading as all arising from the same ancient root words laitho or laithan, meaning way, journey, or 'to travel'?"[109] But journeying with frontline staff is a challenge if we consider the way we hire managers and define management as a culture. We tend to promote high performers into leadership roles instead of leaders. And these newly titled managers, who, only yesterday, were peers with their direct reports, rely more on their previous expertise than the skills of leadership. It was why they were promoted, after all. As a result, they are susceptible to micromanaging their former peers because their previous expertise becomes the new standard for work. Without global standards, managers step in *as the standard*. They are "used to intuiting problems and then telling others how to fix everything."[110] But intuition and declaration is not a real management system.[111]

Sometimes, the best managers know very little about the work they are managing. Although it may seem unusual in our context, it forces curiosity and humility. And allows the leader to focus on leading staff instead of managing the work to be done. It promotes trust in the standard as an objective current best way to do work, not the extension of an overachiever. So, take a moment to reflect on the managers in your organization: were they promoted among peers, or did they follow an unconventional path? Does their leadership ability correlate with your answer?

Let us pause to address the difference between management in Japanese and American companies. Many Lean books inappropriately place the two side by side when they are really comparing apples and oranges. These evaluations are unhelpful since the models are intrinsically different. On the one hand, Japanese managers have an intimate knowledge of the processes of their direct reports. They can train or audit the processes since they are expected to remain experts themselves. But we cannot assume the same for managers in the United States. The manager is an extension of various ancillary teams, including Human Resources (hiring, firing, personnel issues), Finance (budgets, costs, revenue), and Quality. They should have a broad understanding of the Standard Work and Job Description of each role but not the skills or training to do the job itself. Managers can only become leaders when they leave behind the tasks of their subordinates and instead draw their eyes upward to the work that they alone can accomplish. Leaders must be multipliers.

Multiplication is fostered by delegation and stifled by control. Each leader must first recognize and catalog the gifts and talents of her team. This is defined as "discernment" in religious circles. What does each person uniquely bring to the table from their personal, academic, or work background? What sets each person apart? The gaps in a system come next. What current issues, the known-unknowns, or unknown-unknowns, will grow into future barriers for our business? What is most important right now?[112] Delegation is simply a game of matching gifts to needs, putting square pegs in square holes and round pegs in round holes. It is discernment followed by alignment. A leader must always be asking, "who is the right person for this task?"[113] The answer is often the one who can detect issues in a process.[114] Each act of delegation signals to staff that management values their gifts and is willing to make sacrifices for them. Womack describes this as "reciprocal obligation:" Staff are willing to re-invest their gifts into a company once they are first recognized.[115]

Thankfully, management does not rely on willpower alone to transition from control to delegation. Standard work supports the switch.[116] Ishikawa preaches the importance of delegation in his book, *What Is Total Quality Control?*:

> My view is that the task of establishing standardization or setting up regulations should be done in order to delegate authority to subordinates. The key success is to standardize aggressively those things which are plainly understandable and to let a subordinate handle them… The fundamental principle of successful manage-ment is to allow subordinates to make full use of their ability.[117]

The existence of a standard instills confidence in a leader that work can exist beyond her direct circle of influence.

The final step of delegation is getting out of the way. Ishikawa explains, "If things are progressing according to the goals set and according to the standards, then let things be as they are."[118] Imagine a coin spinning on a table. Any attempt to add momentum may disrupt the spinning altogether and is rarely worth the risk. According to Peter Senge, "Managers' funda-mental task is providing the enabling conditions for people to lead the most enriching lives they can."[119] All they must do is trust the system, the stan-dards, and most importantly, the people. The Lean Empowerment System provides a context for the very fulfillment (eudaimonia) Senge references. Not just for staff, but also leaders. Standard Work is just another step on this journey.

Standard Work for Leaders

Leader Standard Work vs. Standard Work for Leaders

Contemporary authors have introduced a new category of Standard Work into Lean literature: "Leader Standard Work."[120] They commonly use the phrase to define the role of leaders going to the Gemba and coaching subordinates through process improvement. Liker summarizes the role as follows: "If we get leaders to go to the Gemba and give them some questions to ask or a checklist of things to look for they will emerge as Lean Leaders."[121] Although this idea and many others have a positive intent, it undersells the impact a manager can make as a Lean leader. This oversimplified notion of Leader Standard Work is makeup on a pig; layering structure and confidence onto a system that is intrinsically unsustainable does nothing to change the underlying system.

A Lean Empowerment System cannot limit leader standard work to tasks associated with the improvement model. It must touch the personal daily work of the leader and simplify their workflows. We must shift our understanding to a more useful model: *Standard work for leaders is different from leader standard work*. The daily work of leaders can and must be standardized to allow them to lead effectively. Because, for many systems, leader standard work is "the missing link."[122] Jim Lancaster, in *The Work of Management*, explains how leaders need "standardized work in order to be consistently useful to each other and to their direct reports."[123] And Peter Hines and Chris Butterworth, in *The Essence of Excellence*, argues how it "generates opportunities to learn for people at all levels of the organization, not just new hires and frontline staff."[124] Let us now turn our attention to standard work for Lean leaders.

Can We Standardize the Work of Leaders?

Consider the Gemba[125] of a manager. It is not the same as frontline staff. The manager splits her time between multiple spaces, both physical and digital. It might be an office tucked away in the building, a conference room, or a hot desk in a centralized location. Digitally speaking, the Gemba is whichever screen is open on the computer. These "locations" may include chat rooms, phone calls, virtual meetings, or the most common of all, an email inbox. The sheer complexity of a leader's Gemba is the very reason why many avoid standardizing a leader's work. Instead, we opt to standardize the work a leader does in *someone else's* Gemba (Leader Standard Work).

Markovitz, in *A Factory of One*, urges each leader to "go to your own Gemba."[126] Miller expands on this idea in *Shingo Principles*: "The most powerful place to begin the process of cultural transformation is with leaders focusing first on their own behaviors... Confronting the realities of your own behaviors is best done at your own *Gemba*."[127] The Gemba of each leader determines the most appropriate form of standard work to fit their needs. The work must fit the context.

Standard work for leaders will look very different at each level of the org chart. Liker explains how each employee has a ratio of task-based work and communication-based work depending on their title. Frontline staff experience a ratio of 90/10 or 80/20 task-based work to communication. Much of their work can be standardized. The shift to a manager comes with a new ratio: 50/50. Communication becomes an integral part of the job, but repetitive tasks can still be standardized.[128] Executive leaders move to a model that places an emphasis on communication over task-based work: 20/80.[129] Strategy becomes the standard for executive leadership. And the focus shifts from content to context.[130]

No matter the rung on the organizational ladder, early attempts to standardize the work of leaders will often be met with resistance. Leaders assume they made it to their role because they rose above the rest of their peers. Some elements of natural variation set them apart and allowed them to excel beyond the standard of their previous role. Now they have earned the right to be a unique leader, distinct from all others. This view will unknowingly cause variation in a system. Leaders begin to act under the "illusion of agreement," assuming their way is the best and right way.[131] Markovitz challenges this notion with an image. Each jazz song is a combination of a steady baseline and improvised rifting. Now imagine a jazz band where every member rifted at the same time and nobody set the baseline.[132] Although rifting is the most revered element of jazz music, a song of pure rifting would no longer fit in the genre. It would be chaos. There must be some baseline for the riffs to stand out. A leader can only provide structure for the riffing of those around them if they hold themselves to a baseline.

To answer the question "Can we standardize the work of leaders," we must be clear about what exactly we can and cannot standardize. We recognize that communication is far more challenging to standardize than tasks, but both demand our attention. We will continue to unpack *communication* and *tasks* in the next two sections.

Communication: Silence the Crying Wolf

Many leaders are addicts, and their drug is unhealthy communication. Our body receives a hit of endorphins from the vibration of a text message or the "ding" of an email. It reminds us that we are needed or valuable to the organization. And we quickly respond, hitting "Reply All" or creating a meeting to discuss the topic. The addiction to vicious cycles of communication is fed by the false platitude "You can't overcommunicate!" And the belief that "all communication is good" can limit our ability to see the waste that results from excess communication. Our fear of deficiency, or failing to communicate, sets an unhelpful precedent for leaders, leading us to layer on more and more. Let this chapter be a support group to help each reader come to terms with our addiction and introduce some guardrails to reduce the wastes of communication.

Waste in the leader's Gemba will look different from waste in the Gemba of frontline staff. It dwells equally, if not more, in the realm of communication and relationships as task-based work. And each one of these wastes is more often revealed as excess instead of deficiency. Let us pretend each email, text, or newsletter is a unit on an assembly line. Next, apply the Lean Production concepts of batching and single piece flow to the units. Those in favor of single piece flow would argue that managers and staff should pass along any bit of information, no matter how small or urgent, to each other as soon as it is received. It may help staff and leaders escalate problems, but at the cost of urgency agnosticism. Everything becomes of equal importance; lunch plans and system-wide outages are both communicated via text message. In contrast, supporters of batching would collect and strategically withhold information until all parties are present in a designated space. Batching reduces the number of times direct reports and leaders need to send emails and one-off messages, with the added risk of failed escalation.

Neither process is fully adequate for communication in a Lean Empowerment System, but we can gather strengths from each. If team members batch information until their weekly team meeting, 90% of messages can wait, whereas the 10% that are truly urgent or need an immediate response can be sent via text, phone call, or email. The same goes for project calls; wait until the project status update call to address any non-urgent matter. Bi-directional batching, with the right system in place, will benefit all parties. Staff and leaders avoid crying wolf about inconsequential topics to save the urgent requests for truly urgent matters.

Batching is only effective if each piece of communication is correctly managed as it sits in waiting. Here we must embrace a method from single piece flow defined by McLoughlin and Miura in *True Kaizen* as "first in first out" or "FIFO." In their words, "if something is not ready to be worked on, it needs to be stored elsewhere, not on the shop floor, so that items get worked on in the order they are received onto the shop floor, not into the system in general."[133] *We must find a home for each piece of communication, either queued up for immediate action, or batched in a safe and organized space.* Again, the only risk is the gradual decay of urgency when a piece of information is surrounded by other pieces of information that have less bearing on strategy. Imai warns that information can "rot" when not passed to the right person in a system or passed at the right time.[134]

Let us consider one final tool from Lean Production Systems to help us transform communication: Push and Pull systems. Just as assembly lines pull product when ready instead of the previous station piling up inventory to be worked, staff in both leadership and frontline roles are better served when they can pull communication instead of pushing it. But there is the rub: It is not realistic to ask staff what they will need before they need it. This is like expecting patients to know the healthcare they will need next year. And leaders may not have relevant content to share until pressures increase from other sources or messaging trickles down from their leaders. For the most real-time communication, we must rely on both feed-back and feed-forward loops.[135] Striking a balance between these two loops is the best way to triage problems as they arise.[136] If we truly believe "the next process is the customer," then we must feed-forward as much as necessary for the team to succeed.

Finally, as with everything else in the Lean Empowerment System, the goal of improvement is an increased respect for people. Over time, as staff feel empowered to do tasks instead of pushing them to a manager, the amount of shared work between leader and staff will increase. And the more that staff feel comfortable batching, the more empowered they are to react creatively on their own. A telling symbol of company culture is how easily staff can make a decision without going up a layer on the org chart.[137] Take a moment to reflect on the Cc lists of the emails in your inbox. How many include staff from two or more layers of the org chart?

I hope this section has convinced you that it is possible to standardize or at least simplify the communication-based parts of a leader's job. Our leaders, from managers to C-Suite executives, are drowning in communication without ever having received a basic swimming lesson. Many think they are Michael Phelps but are doggy paddling in circles. We must not assume that our leaders know healthy communication patterns that empower both them and frontline staff. It must be added to the core framework and education of Lean Empowerment. With this lesson in mind, we can turn our attention to the tasks that form a necessary part of management.

Tasks: Checklists and Visual Task Boards

Look around your workplace and observe how many leaders still use paper notepads or planners to manage their tasks. It seems like everything else in our world has evolved. Why hasn't our personal work management? Now think about the training options for leaders on the topic of personal work management. I am personally not aware of any organization that orients staff how to manage their tasks. Why do we blindly assume the highest paid individuals in an organization are equipped to efficiently complete their work? Let us review the pervasiveness of paper to-do lists and propose a new model for personal work management that increases our capacity for fulfillment and conserves energy for empowerment.

First, an effective system of personal work management must produce control. And according to Benson and Barry, authors of *Personal Kanban* and advocates for improved personal work management, "Work unseen is work uncontrolled."[138] Any new tool we propose must help leaders visualize problems and prioritize work.[139] Although this may not seem revolutionary, we must only glance at the vast quantity of handwritten notes taken on the back of meeting agendas or in the margins of a notebook to know it is something we lack. It is impossible for a leader to visualize all their work if it lives in many places across a myriad of physical and digital tools. And the psychological toll is heavy; the self-induced chaos of hunting down notes and tasks and names does not instill within leaders the confidence of control. Instead, it keeps us up at night.

An efficient and confident leader consolidates all her tasks into one place. This is the basic definition of a checklist. Markovitz expands with a similar definition: "transform complex, creative work into simple, 'transactional' tasks that can be easily done."[140] Juran also defines a checklist as "an aid to human memory – a reminder of what to do and what not to do."[141] And although checklists are rudimentary, they are valuable.[142] Basic versions are akin to a grocery list or sticky note reminder, while complexity can vary from spreadsheets to project plans. Each one is somewhat boring and supports regimentation, but that is the point. Personal work management isn't rocket science, but rocket science depends on it.[143]

Although basic checklists are useful, they are only the first step toward comprehensive work management. We must follow their evolution one step further into the visual task board, also known as Daily Management or a kanban board.[144] Visual task boards are commonly used by teams that receive and conduct their work according to tickets submitted by internal or external customers. Each task is treated as a separate "ticket" that contains all the details required to meet the success criteria. Teams can easily assign tasks, visualize team capacity and throughput, and understand progress toward a goal. The task lifecycle starts in the Backlog (to-do), moves to In Progress, and finally to Complete. And the entire board is malleable, adapting to the needs of the user and her responsibilities. The tangible progression of an idea to completion gives immediate feedback to the person responsible.

A visual task board is unique in that it provides lessons learned in live time to the user. Although experiences will vary, most organizations do not take time to review lessons learned or apply the learnings to future initiatives. And even if a reflection process is hardcoded in an organization's project management structure, the likelihood of it happening in personal work management is slim. But the application of visual task boards will provide immediate feedback to users. Each person can immediately see which types of tasks they are drawn to completing quickly versus those tasks that linger until one musters enough energy to start them. This process can help budding leaders understand their gifts and gaps. It is another form of discernment.

It is also important that we not confuse throughput with capacity.[145] According to Benson and Barry, capacity is a *spatial relationship*, like water in a cup. "Capacity is an ineffective measure of throughput, and a horrible way to gauge what we can do. It doesn't measure how we actually work, or at what rate we actually work. Capacity is a mere brute force measure of what will fit."[146] It should not be used to measure human work, yet leaders insist on using capacity to define the capability of their team.

But staff are ultimately as capable as their system allows, not containers to be filled with work. This is where the measurement of capacity falls short. For example, philosophies of capacity plague the realm of education. According to this dated idea, the brains of students are empty containers that must be filled with knowledge bestowed by the teacher. Students do not actively participate in the learning process and are dependent on others for knowledge.

Throughput is a better way to define human work since it is a *flow relationship*, like cars on a highway. "Throughput is a flow-based system. It measures success by the amount of quality work flowing from READY to DONE over time, not just the volume of work we can cram into our schedule."[147] Imagine a Ferrari and a bicycle in a traffic jam; it doesn't matter how fast they can go if they are both limited by the throughput of the system. Underperformers and overachievers working at the same level is the telltale sign of throughput flowing at its finest – not hard work, previous education, or training. Because our workforce is not home to Ferraris and bicycles, rockstars and underperformers; it is composed of people who are doing the best they can with the resources they have been given.

It is important to be clear about one point before moving forward: the evolution from checklists to a visual task board will feel like additional work until the "new normal" becomes as habitual as the previous process. Leaders must be patient to overcome initial discouragement. Things will feel worse before they feel better. Because, according to Juran, "To go full scale into annual quality improvement adds about 10 percent to the work load of the entire management team, including the upper managers."[148] Any proposal for improvement must overcome the hesitation of staff based on historical "improvements" that never felt better after they felt worse. Countless leaders have promised the greener grass of efficiency on the other side of change, but few have followed through to the extent that personal work management can promise.

Productive Forgetfulness

Many leaders are desperate to leave work at work and devote their full attention at home to family or personal life. Burnout and pajama time, time spent working outside of work hours, are at an all-time high, which has led to an increased demand for efficiency of practice.[149] But we cannot realistically drop everything when we get in our car or close our laptop (we will explore this idea further in Chapter 7). Instead, we must find ways to be just productive and forgetful enough to fully invest in both areas of our lives. Any effective personal work management system must allow leaders to purposefully and productively forget certain things with the full trust that they can return to them as needed. This idea is at the core of Lean, and the reason why Toyoda simplified the loom before entering the world of car production. He wanted his mom, a weaver, to have a more enjoyable life, free from the frustrations caused by inefficient processes.[150] His rationale was simple: make today better than yesterday.[151] We learn from his powerful example how the reduction of waste can make room for fulfillment both at work and at home.

The Lean Empowerment System is ultimately concerned with the psychological health of each employee and the perception of control that a personal work management system can first create and continuously improve. Let us break down our newly coined definition of productive forgetfulness into three categories:

- My Tasks
- Others' Tasks for Me
- Content

My Tasks

The human brain is a funny thing. We convince ourselves that we can work on multiple things at once, remember everything on our plate, and simply turn off our brain when we leave work. Instead of fueling these false ideas that are ingrained in Western society, I encourage us to embrace our natural struggle to focus, our forgetfulness, and our anxiety about incomplete work. We can only propose a new standard process for personal work management once we acknowledge our limits.

Unfocused

First, we must realize that our brains cannot multi-task. The phrase itself is a fault of the English language. It is misleading and makes an empty promise. Multi-tasking should be called "switch-tasking" since our minds switch from thing to thing rapidly as new stimuli appear.[152] Let us understand the gravity of this statement with an image: Pretend you are checking emails while listening to a meeting through a headset. Now imagine your eyes blinking each time your focus shifts from the conversation in your ear to the words on your screen. Do you think your eyes would remain open long enough to ever focus on reading a single email? This type of self-induced task-thrashing will exhaust our brain, interfere with productivity, and lower quality. And it's not like we do this on accident; we wear it as a badge of honor and brag about our ability to stretch our focus.

Single piece flow is the antidote for the illusion of multi-tasking. We must productively forget about all the other work on our plate to focus on the one task at hand. But we must be clear that we are not neglecting the other work, simply storing it until we are ready to give it our undivided attention. Recall the theory of First In First Out (FIFO), which places work not currently being worked in a place away from the assembly line. For knowledge workers, the visual task board (Kanban) is the most effective tool to help us visualize our backlog and limit our work in progress. Kanban boards lose their meaning in the absence of single piece flow.[153] Its true purpose is to help leaders pull work from its home at the appropriate time.[154] This is akin to the definition of time as *Kairos*, or the "right time."

Forgetful

The human brain has trouble remembering more than a handful of topics at one time. We are forgetful by nature and must acknowledge this hard truth to set ourselves up for success. Shingo explains how there are two kinds of forgetfulness that we must be aware of. The first is basic forgetfulness and overlooking things. The second is "forgetting that we might forget" or "when we forget to make sure that we have not overlooked something."[155] He argues that checklists and error-proofing (Poka-Yoke) are the best ways to avoid forgetfulness. He is essentially arguing in favor of productive forgetfulness.

Anxious

When our brain is not switch-tasking or forgetting, it is probably tripping over itself with incomplete thoughts. The Zeigarnik Effect "states that adults have a 90% chance of remembering interrupted and incomplete thoughts or actions over those that have been seen through to completion… the brain becomes preoccupied with missing pieces of information. Unfinished tasks vie for our attention, causing intrusive thoughts that ultimately impede productivity and increase the opportunity for error."[156] Think of the last time you had a breakthrough idea: did it happen in the shower, on a walk, or in the car? Our best thinking occurs when we are in a state of rest, labeled by neuroscientists as the default mode. Our brain forms new neuropathways between seemingly unlike ideas, across disciplines or even languages, to form innovative solutions. But this state is only possible when incomplete thoughts are completed or productively forgotten. We can increase our likelihood of activating the default mode by reducing the anxiety caused by open tasks.

The Zeigarnik Effect has a very real impact on our mood and daily inter-actions. For example, my wife and I purchased a house that needed signifi-cant renovations. The garage was our designated workshop and temporary home to sawhorses, miter saw, paint supplies, and any other tool that was too messy for indoors. Our contractors also made themselves at home in the space, littering the floor with cardboard boxes and drop cloths. We accepted the mess as a necessary evil and steppingstone to our dream home.

Each morning I walked through the garage to my car, trying hard not to trip. I passed through the same space later in the day after my commute home and before seeing my family inside. I thought nothing of this simple regimen until I decided one day to exit my house through the front door. Although I didn't have a blood pressure cuff available to prove it, I entered my car and office with a heightened sense of peace. The same applied to my arrival home; I reacted to my family with more patience and less anxiety.

Once the renovations were complete and contractors paid, I convinced my wife to let us invest in making our garage a clean and organized space. I knew the impact it would have on two of the most important transitions of my day. Similarly, we experience a "cluttered garage" every time we remember work in progress outside of the appropriate time to address them. Personal work management is the best remedy for these unwanted anxious thoughts.

Others' Tasks for Me

Over time I have learned that roughly one-third of my personal to-dos are dependent on the work of others. And I discovered the hard way that others are not ultimately responsible for the outcome of the tasks; I am. The next step in personal work management is setting up a mechanism to track and follow-up with others on the one-third of your work that depends on them.

Now I encourage you to answer this next question with as little delusion as possible: What percent of the time do people do a task when you first ask them? I have asked this question to over 150+ leaders and am consistently surprised by their response. The average response ranges from 15 to 25% of the time. The most optimistic response I received was 50% from a co-worker who is literally a saint in human flesh. Now pause for a minute. This should be alarming. Roughly one-third of our work is entrusted to the responsibility of others, and only one-quarter of the time do they get back without additional prompting. We are in big trouble if we lack a system to document, monitor, and nudge others.

Digital versions of visual task boards can flag users to review a task when a due date is passed. This is an example of a reflexive system, more commonly known as a "trip-wire," that triggers an alert when certain criteria are met.[157] Before learning the magnitude of the problem stated above, I never tracked the work that others owed me. But now, I encourage anyone, as part of their personal work management, to create a task every time they ask for something to be done.[158] Don't bet on the odds of others following through. Simply put the person's name, the task, and set the due date out one week in the future (or less if the task is more urgent). Then ignore it. Forget you ever asked. You might be pleasantly surprised (25% of the time) to receive an answer. Simply check off the reminder. But more likely than not (75% of the time), you'll be reminded in a week to reach back out. Everyone appreciates a gentle reminder, or "Hey, have you had an opportunity to review my request from last week?" And I bet you the response rate after the first reminder is met with 100% success within the day.

Sharing accountability with a team increases respect for others and hastens the improvement process. It accepts the realistic nature of humans as unfocused, forgetful, and anxious, and offers an olive branch to our neighbor in times of need. And, as more and more users adopt personal work management systems, entire organizational cultures will shift towards increased accountability. Adding a task in front of another person instills confidence that work will actually get done, whereas jotting down a note on paper is met with distrust. People will joke in meetings, "should I add that to my to-do, or can you just remind me in a week?" Accountability and follow-through must regain its rightful place as a basic human right in the workplace.

What Should I Forget? Search Engine

Take a second to think: do you remember the four vices of management and the corresponding vices of empowerment from Chapter 1? It is ok if you don't because you have this book as a reference. But the likelihood of you remembering the answer to my question is correlative to the generation in which you received elementary education. Older generations were taught in school to memorize content more often than younger generations. This is partly due to the Internet and Search Engines. We have shifted our educational models away from mnemonic devices, songs, and acronyms to the study of SEO (search engine optimization) that emphasizes keywords and algorithms. Even Elmo on Sesame Street consults his floating smartphone friend, Smartie, with the question: "Well, what do we do to learn something new? We… look it up!" This shift in thinking has also broken into the workplace, but less people are aware of it.

My younger brother (Gen Z), who is only seven years younger than me, does not know a world without internet search engines. Millennials, like me, are at the cusp of the search engine way of thinking; we are fluent in computer usage but recall a time before search engines. Nowadays the idea of a card catalog in a library is somewhat silly and archaic. It is limited to the resources available at the library and the knowledge of the librarian. But now the problem isn't the lack of resources. It's quite the opposite! A new skill is learning how to wade through vast quantities of knowledge to find something reputable and relevant.

Unless you are one of the gifted few with photographic memory, we must do our human nature a favor and start to trust search engines. I have learned through my coaching of leaders that the fear associated with removing emails from an Inbox is our fear of losing them. We are worried that we cannot find them later. But I am quick to remind people that every popular email software now has a robust search engine built into the tool-bar. The same goes for file storage in the cloud. The seemingly endless expanse of cloud-based storage is not as overwhelming because of the search engine technology that keeps pace. Therefore, the fear of losing information is no longer a valid argument against improving our personal work management. Our clutter no longer has an excuse.

Sherlock Holmes, in *A Study in Scarlet*, tells Watson, "Consider that a man's brain originally is like a little empty attic, and you have to stock it with such furniture as you choose." Holmes was known to only store information, or in this case, furniture, that could one day be helpful. The rest was discarded. We must also challenge what is needed in our brains versus at our fingertips. Every "how" or "what" in our brain must be accompanied by a "why" or it clutters space that could be filled with "who." We fast from memorization and rely on search engines to feast on relationships.

A checklist or visual task board can help standardize repeatable work to let our leaders funnel creative energy into non-repeatable work.[159] This promise is attractive to many leaders who want to leave behind task work and focus on strategy, communication, and connection, which are perceived by many as the "work of leaders." Any step that a leader takes in the direction of standardization is a step toward freedom. The more work we can productively forget, the more room we free up to be compassionate.

Notes

1 Brenda Zimmerman, Curt Lindberg & Paul Plsek, *Edgeware: Lessons from Complexity Science for Health Care Leaders* (IIrving, Texas V H A, Incorporated, 2008), 174.

2 Collin McLoughlin & Toshihiko Miura, *True Kaizen: Management's Role in Improving Work Climate and Culture* (Boca Raton, FL: CRC, 2018), 22.

3 Masaaki Imai, *Kaizen (ky'zen): The Key to Japan's Competitive Success* (New York City, NY: McGraw-Hill, 1991), 15.

4 Ibid., xxix.

5 Ibid.

6 Ibid., xxxi.

7 Please note: We are not talking about a Feedback Loop in Systems Thinking language which focuses on corrective processes and stabilizing processes [Donella H. Meadows, *Thinking in Systems* (Chelsea, VT: Chelsea Green Publishing, 2008), 26-7.]

8 Joseph E. Swartz & Mark Graban, *Healthcare Kaizen: Engaging Front-Line Staff in Sustainable Continuous Improvements* (Boca Raton, FL: CRC Press), 33.

9 Ibid., 32.

10 J. M. Juran, *Juran on Leadership for Quality: An Executive Handbook* (Florence, MA: Free Press, 1989), 146.

11 Daniel Markovitz, *Building the Fit Organization: Six Core Principles for Making Your Company Stronger, Faster, and More Competitive* (New York: McGraw-Hill Education, 2016), 32.

12 J. M. Juran, *Juran on Leadership for Quality: An Executive Handbook* (Florence, MA: Free Press, 1989), 283.

13 Ibid., 287.

14 Ibid., 264.

15 Daniel Markovitz, *Building the Fit Organization: Six Core Principles for Making Your Company Stronger, Faster, and More Competitive* (New York: McGraw-Hill Education, 2016), 81-83.

16 Masaaki Imai, *Kaizen (ky'zen): The Key to Japan's Competitive Success* (New York City, NY: McGraw-Hill, 1991), 112.

17 Timothy R. Clark, *The 4 Stages of Psychological Safety: Defining the Path to Inclusion and Innovation* (Oakland, CA: Berrett-Koehler Publishers, Inc., 2020), 13.

18 Baer, M., & Frese, M. (2003). Innovation is not enough: Climates for initiative and psychological safety, process innovations, and firm performance. *Journal of Organizational Behavior, 24*(1), 50.

19 Alfie Kohn, *Punished by rewards: The trouble with gold stars, incentive plans, A's, praise, and other bribes* (Boston, MA: Mariner Books, 1993), 115.

20 Timothy R. Clark, *The 4 Stages of Psychological Safety: Defining the Path to Inclusion and Innovation* (Oakland, CA: Berrett-Koehler Publishers, Inc., 2020), 136.

21 For a History of Psychological safety, see Amy C. Edmondson, *The Fearless Organization: Creating Psychological Safety in the Workplace for Learning, Innovation, and Growth* (Hoboken, NJ: John Wiley & Sons, 2019), xviii.

22 Ibid., 47.

23 Baer, M., & Frese, M. (2003). Innovation is not enough: Climates for initiative and psychological safety, process innovations, and firm performance. *Journal of Organizational Behavior, 24*(1), 49, 57.

24 Alfie Kohn, *Punished by Rewards: The Trouble with Gold Stars, Incentive Plans, A's, Praise, and Other Bribes* (Boston, MA: Mariner Books, 1993), 253.

25 Robert Miller, *Hearing the Voice of the Shingo Principles: Creating Sustainable Cultures of Enterprise Excellence* (Abingdon, Oxfordshire: Routledge, 2018), 96.

26 W. Edwards Deming, *Out of the Crisis* (Cambridge, MA: The MIT Press, 2018), 338.

27 Amy C. Edmondson, *The Fearless Organization: Creating Psychological Safety in the Workplace for Learning, Innovation, and Growth* (Hoboken, NJ: John Wiley & Sons, 2019), xvi, W. H. Baker & K. D. Rolfes, *Lean for the Long Term: Sustainment is a Myth, Transformation Is Reality* (New York, NY: Productivity Press, 2017), 34.

28 Alfie Kohn, *Punished by Rewards: The Trouble with Gold Stars, Incentive Plans, A's, Praise, and Other Bribes* (Boston, MA: Mariner Books, 1993), 195.

29 Brenda Zimmerman, Curt Lindberg & Paul Plsek, *Edgeware: Lessons from Complexity Science for Health Care Leaders* (Irving, Texas V H A, Incorporated, 2008), 68.

30 Amy C. Edmondson, *The Fearless Organization: Creating Psychological Safety in the Workplace for Learning, Innovation, and Growth* (Hoboken, NJ: John Wiley & Sons, 2019), xvi.

31 https://hbr.org/2016/01/can-your-employees-really-speak-freely

32 Masaaki Imai, *Kaizen (ky'zen): The Key to Japan's Competitive Success* (New York City, NY: McGraw-Hill, 1991), 113.

33 Donald Dinero, *Training Within Industry: The Foundation of Lean* (New York, NY: Productivity Press, 2005), 59.

34 Masaaki Imai, *Kaizen (ky'zen): The Key to Japan's Competitive Success* (New York City, NY: McGraw-Hill, 1991), 15.

35 https://hbr.org/2021/09/what-evolution-can-teach-us-about-innovation

36 Masaaki Imai, *Kaizen (ky'zen): The Key to Japan's Competitive Success* (New York City, NY: McGraw-Hill, 1991), 15.

37 Alfie Kohn, *Punished by Rewards: The Trouble with Gold Stars, Incentive Plans, A's, Praise, and Other Bribes* (Boston, MA: Mariner Books, 1993), 87.

38 Ibid., 89.

39 Donald Dinero, *Training Within Industry: The Foundation of Lean* (New York, NY: Productivity Press, 2005), 249.

40 Alfie Kohn, *Punished by Rewards: The Trouble with Gold Stars, Incentive Plans, A's, Praise, and Other Bribes* (Boston, MA: Mariner Books, 1993), 48.

41 Ibid., 56.

42 Ibid., 187.

43 Thomas L. Jackson, *Standard Work for Lean Healthcare (Lean Tools For Healthcare Series)* (New York, NY: Productivity Press, 2011), 38.

44 Ibid., 48.
45 Jeffrey K. Liker & George Trachilis, *Developing Lean Leaders at All Levels: A Practical Guide* (Jacksonville, FL: Lean Leadership Institute Publications, 2014), 101.
46 Daniel Kahneman, Olivier Sibony, & Cass R. Sunstein, *Noise: A Flaw in Human Judgment* (Boston, MA: Little, Brown Spark, 2021), 12.
47 Ibid., 53.
48 Geoffrey West, *Scale: The Universal Laws of Life, Growth, and Death in Organisms, Cities, and Companies* (London: Penguin Books, 2018), 89.
49 W. Edwards Deming, *The New Economics: For Industry, Government, Education* (Cambridge, MA: The MIT Press, 2018), 98.
50 Daniel Kahneman, Olivier Sibony, & Cass R. Sunstein, *Noise: A Flaw in Human Judgment* (Boston, MA: Little, Brown Spark, 2021), 15.
51 J. M. Juran, *Managerial Breakthrough* (New York, NY: McGraw-Hill Book Co., 1995), 41.
52 Productivity Press Development Team, *Standard Work for the Shopfloor (The Shopfloor Series)* (New York, NY: Productivity Press, 2002), 7.
53 Thomas L. Jackson, *Standard Work for Lean Healthcare (Lean Tools For Healthcare Series)* (New York, NY: Productivity Press, 2011), 39.
54 Daniel Kahneman, Olivier Sibony, & Cass R. Sunstein, *Noise: A Flaw in Human Judgment* (Boston, MA: Little, Brown Spark, 2021), 358.
55 Robert Miller, *Hearing the Voice of the Shingo Principles: Creating Sustainable Cultures of Enterprise Excellence* (Abingdon, Oxfordshire: Routledge, 2018), 118.
56 Masaaki Imai, *Kaizen (ky'zen): The Key to Japan's Competitive Success* (New York City, NY: McGraw-Hill, 1991), 63-4.
57 Ibid.
58 W. Edwards Deming, *Out of the Crisis* (Cambridge, MA: The MIT Press, 2018), 338.
59 Richard Bohmer, *Designing Care: Aligning Nature and Management of Health Care* (Boston, MA: Harvard Business Review Press, 2009), 170.
60 Jim Lancaster, *The Work of Management: A Daily Path to Sustainable Improvement* (Cambridge, MA: Lean Enterprise Institute Inc., 2017), 154.
61 Productivity Press Development Team, *Standard Work for the Shopfloor (The Shopfloor Series)* (New York, NY: Productivity Press, 2002), 72.
62 Daniel Kahneman, Olivier Sibony, & Cass R. Sunstein, *Noise: A Flaw in Human Judgment* (Boston, MA: Little, Brown Spark, 2021), 356.
63 W. Edwards Deming, *Out of the Crisis* (Cambridge, MA: The MIT Press, 2018), 298.
64 Daniel Kahneman, Olivier Sibony, & Cass R. Sunstein, *Noise: A Flaw in Human Judgment* (Boston, MA: Little, Brown Spark, 2021), 357.
65 Brenda Zimmerman, Curt Lindberg & Paul Plsek, *Edgeware: Lessons from Complexity Science for Health Care Leaders* (Irving, Texas V H A, Incorporated, 2008), 70.

66 Daniel Markovitz, *A Factory of One: Applying Lean Principles to Banish Waste and Improve your Personal Performance* (Boca Raton: CRC Press, 2012), 125.

67 Daniel Markovitz, *Building the Fit Organization: Six Core Principles for Making Your Company Stronger, Faster, and More Competitive* (New York: McGraw-Hill Education, 2016), 92.

68 Clayton Christensen, J. H. Grossman & J. Hwang, *The Innovator's Prescription: A Disruptive Solution for Health Care* (New York, NY: McGraw-Hill Education, 2017), 38.

69 Patrick Graupp & Martha Purrier, *Getting to Standard Work in Health Care: Using TWI to Create a Foundation for Quality Care.* (New York, NY: Productivity Press, 2022), 20, 26.

70 W. Edwards Deming, *Out of the Crisis* (Cambridge, MA: The MIT Press, 2018), 11.

71 James Clear, *Atomic Habits: An Easy & Proven Way to Build Good Habits & Break Bad Ones* (New York, NY: Avery Publishing, 2018), 46.

72 Daniel Markovitz, *Building the Fit Organization: Six Core Principles for Making Your Company Stronger, Faster, and More Competitive* (New York: McGraw-Hill Education, 2016), 107-108.

73 Emily Adams & John Toussaint, *Management on the Mend: The Healthcare Executive Guide to System Transformation* (Appleton, WI: ThedaCare Center for Healthcare Value, 2015), 112.

74 Ibid., 142.

75 Daniel Markovitz, *Building the Fit Organization: Six Core Principles for Making Your Company Stronger, Faster, and More Competitive* (New York, NY: McGraw-Hill Education, 2016), 124.

76 James Clear, *Atomic Habits: An Easy & Proven Way to Build Good Habits & Break Bad Ones* (New York, NY: Avery Publishing, 2018), 16.

77 Ibid., 92.

78 Peter Hines & Chris Butterworth, *The Essence of Excellence: Creating a Culture of Continuous Improvement* (Caerphilly, United Kingdom: S A Partners, 2019), 23.

79 W. Edwards Deming, *Out of the Crisis* (Cambridge, MA: The MIT Press, 2018), 11.

80 James Clear, *Atomic Habits: An Easy & Proven Way to Build Good Habits & Break Bad Ones* (New York, NY: Avery Publishing, 2018), 90.

81 J. M. Juran, *Managerial Breakthrough* (New York, NY: McGraw-Hill Book Co., 1995), 269.

82 Batalden, Paul B et al. Microsystems in health care: Part 5. How leaders are leading. *Joint Commission journal on quality and safety* vol. 29,6 (2003): 303. doi:10.1016/s1549-3741(03)29034-1

83 Peter Valenzuela. Rational Numbers. Group Practice Journal, July/August 2022, 12.

84 Alfie Kohn, *Punished by rewards: The Trouble with Gold Stars, Incentive Plans, A's, Praise, and Other Bribes* (Boston, MA: Mariner Books, 1993), 115.

85 Kaoru Ishikawa, *What is Total Quality Control? The Japanese Way* (1985), 8.

86 Ibid., 44.

87 W. Edwards Deming, *Out of the Crisis* (Cambridge, MA: The MIT Press, 2018), 299.

88 Patrick Graupp & Martha Purrier, *Getting to Standard Work in Health Care: Using TWI to Create a Foundation for Quality Care.* (New York, NY: Productivity Press, 2022), 103. Theories from TWI argue that standards are "not particularly useful for training." Instead we need Job Instruction Breakdown Sheets that highlight important steps, key points, and reasons, without a comprehensive step-by-step description. Leaders can choose to use Standard Work in training or create a summary version as long as the standard remains the source of truth.

89 J. M. Juran, *Juran on Leadership for Quality: An Executive Handbook* (Florence, MA: Free Press, 1989), 304.

90 Joseph E. Swartz & Mark Graban, *Healthcare Kaizen: Engaging Front-Line Staff in Sustainable Continuous Improvements* (Boca Raton, FL: CRC Press), 149.

91 Timothy R. Clark, *The 4 Stages of Psychological Safety: Defining the Path to Inclusion and Innovation* (Oakland, CA: Berrett-Koehler Publishers, Inc., 2020), 45.

92 Amy C. Edmondson, *The Fearless Organization: Creating Psychological Safety in the Workplace for Learning, Innovation, and Growth* (Hoboken, NJ: John Wiley & Sons, 2019), 167.

93 Collin McLoughlin & Toshihiko Miura, *True Kaizen: Management's Role in Improving Work Climate and Culture* (Boca Raton, FL: CRC, 2018), 74.

94 https://hbr.org/2016/01/can-your-employees-really-speak-freely

95 J. M. Juran, *Juran on Leadership for Quality: An Executive Handbook* (Florence, MA: Free Press, 1989), 100.

96 Amy C. Edmondson, *The Fearless Organization: Creating Psychological Safety in the Workplace for Learning, Innovation, and Growth* (Hoboken, NJ: John Wiley & Sons, 2019), 31.

97 Masaaki Imai, *Kaizen (ky'zen): The Key to Japan's Competitive Success* (New York City, NY: McGraw-Hill, 1991), 163.

98 Thomas Graham, *Innovation the Cleveland Clinic Way: Powering Transformation by Putting Ideas to Work* (New York, NY: McGraw-Hill Education, 2016), 19.

99 Timothy R. Clark, *The 4 Stages of Psychological Safety: Defining the Path to Inclusion and Innovation* (Oakland, CA: Berrett-Koehler Publishers, Inc., 2020), 119.

100 Kaoru Ishikawa, *What is Total Quality Control? The Japanese Way* (1985), 82.

101 Timothy R. Clark, *The 4 Stages of Psychological Safety: Defining the Path to Inclusion and Innovation* (Oakland, CA: Berrett-Koehler Publishers, Inc., 2020), 12.

102 Emily Adams & John Toussaint, *Management on the Mend: The Healthcare Executive Guide to System Transformation* (Appleton, WI: ThedaCare Center for Healthcare Value, 2015), 87.

103 https://www.google.com/amp/s/www.nytimes.com/2020/01/06/smarter-living/how-to-complain-.amp.html

104 Collin McLoughlin & Toshihiko Miura, *True Kaizen: Management's Role in Improving Work Climate and Culture* (Boca Raton, FL: CRC, 2018), 198.

105 James R. Detert and Ethan Burris https://hbr.org/2016/01/can-your-employees-really-speak-freely

106 Timothy R. Clark, *The 4 Stages of Psychological Safety: Defining the Path to Inclusion and Innovation* (Oakland, CA: Berrett-Koehler Publishers, Inc., 2020), 13.

107 W. Edwards Deming, *Out of the Crisis* (Cambridge, MA: The MIT Press, 2018), 248.

108 William Sherkenbach, *Deming's Road to Continual Improvement* (Knoxville, TN: Statistical Process Control Press, 1991), 92.

109 Batalden, Paul B et al. Microsystems in health care: Part 5. How leaders are leading. *Joint Commission journal on quality and safety* vol. 297 (2003): 303. doi:10.1016/s1549-3741(03)29034-1

110 Masaaki Imai, *Kaizen (ky'zen): The Key to Japan's Competitive Success* (New York City, NY: McGraw-Hill, 1991), 77.

111 Emily Adams & John Toussaint, *Management on the Mend: The Healthcare Executive Guide to System Transformation* (Appleton, WI: ThedaCare Center for Healthcare Value, 2015), 93.

112 Patrick Lencioni, *The Advantage: Why Organizational Health Trumps Everything Else in Business* (San Francisco, CA: Jossey-Bass, 2012).

113 Patrick Graupp & Martha Purrier, *Getting to Standard Work in Health Care: Using TWI to Create a Foundation for Quality Care.* (New York, NY: Productivity Press, 2022), 53.

114 Collin McLoughlin & Toshihiko Miura, *True Kaizen: Management's Role in Improving Work Climate and Culture* (Boca Raton, FL: CRC, 2018), 156-7.

115 James Womack, Daniel Jones, & Daniel Roos, *The Machine That Changed the World* (Manhattan, NY: Simon & Schuster, 2007), 100.

116 Thomas L. Jackson, *Standard Work for Lean Healthcare (Lean Tools For Healthcare Series)* (New York, NY: Productivity Press, 2011), 75.

117 Kaoru Ishikawa, *What is Total Quality Control? The Japanese Way* (1985), 65, 112.

118 Ibid., 67.

119 Peter Senge, *The Fifth Discipline* (Manhattan, NY: Random House Business, 2006), 130.

120 Peter Hines & Chris Butterworth, *The Essence of Excellence: Creating a Culture of Continuous Improvement* (Caerphilly, United Kingdom: S A Partners, 2019), 129.

121 Jeffrey K. Liker & George Trachilis, *Developing Lean Leaders at All Levels: A Practical Guide* (Jacksonville, FL: Lean Leadership Institute Publications, 2014), 197.

122 Peter Hines & Chris Butterworth, *The Essence of Excellence: Creating a Culture of Continuous Improvement* (Caerphilly, United Kingdom: S A Partners, 2019), 163.

123 Jim Lancaster, *The Work of Management: A Daily Path to Sustainable Improvement* (Cambridge, MA: Lean Enterprise Institute Inc., 2017), 64.

124 "the actual place where work is done".

125 Peter Hines & Chris Butterworth, *The Essence of Excellence: Creating a Culture of Continuous Improvement* (Caerphilly, United Kingdom: S A Partners, 2019), 167.

126 Daniel Markovitz, *A Factory of One: Applying Lean Principles to Banish Waste and Improve your Personal Performance* (Boca Raton: CRC Press, 2012), 10.

127 Robert Miller, *Hearing the Voice of the Shingo Principles: Creating Sustainable Cultures of Enterprise Excellence* (Abingdon, Oxfordshire: Routledge, 2018), 89.

128 Peter Hines & Chris Butterworth, *The Essence of Excellence: Creating a Culture of Continuous Improvement* (Caerphilly, United Kingdom: S A Partners, 2019), 127-8.

129 Jeffrey K. Liker & George Trachilis, *Developing Lean Leaders at All Levels: A Practical Guide* (Jacksonville, FL: Lean Leadership Institute Publications, 2014), 198.

130 Harvard Business Review, *HBR Guide to Getting the Mentoring You Need (HBR Guide Series)* (Boston, MA: Harvard Business Review Press, 2014), 2.

131 Daniel Kahneman, Olivier Sibony, & Cass R. Sunstein, *Noise: A Flaw in Human Judgment* (Boston, MA: Little, Brown Spark, 2021), 30.

132 Daniel Markovitz, *A Factory of One: Applying Lean Principles to Banish Waste and Improve your Personal Performance* (Boca Raton: CRC Press, 2012), 141.

133 Collin McLoughlin & Toshihiko Miura, *True Kaizen: Management's Role in Improving Work Climate and Culture* (Boca Raton, FL: CRC, 2018), 159.

134 Masaaki Imai, *Kaizen (ky'zen): The Key to Japan's Competitive Success* (New York City, NY: McGraw-Hill, 1991), 93.

135 Kosnik, Linda K, and James A Espinosa. Microsystems in health care: Part 7. The microsystem as a platform for merging strategic planning and operations. *Joint Commission journal on quality and safety* vol. 29,9 (2003): 453. doi:10.1016/s1549-3741(03)29054-7.

136 Shingeo Shingo, *A Study of the Toyota Production System* (Boca Raton, FL: Routledge, 1989), 178.

137 Collin McLoughlin & Toshihiko Miura, *True Kaizen: Management's Role in Improving Work Climate and Culture* (Boca Raton, FL: CRC, 2018), 2.

138 Jim Benson & Tonianne Demaria Barry, *Personal Kanban; Mapping Work, Navigating Life* (Seattle, WA: Modus Cooperandi Press, 2011), 152.

139 Productivity Press Development Team, *Standard Work for the Shopfloor (The Shopfloor Series)* (New York, NY: Productivity Press, 2002), 17.

140 Daniel Markovitz, *A Factory of One: Applying Lean Principles to Banish Waste and Improve your Personal Performance* (Boca Raton: CRC Press, 2012), 75.

141 J. M. Juran, *Juran on Leadership for Quality: An Executive Handbook* (Florence, MA: Free Press, 1989), 140.

142 Daniel Markovitz, *Building the Fit Organization: Six Core Principles for Making Your Company Stronger, Faster, and More Competitive* (New York: McGraw-Hill Education, 2016), 90.

143 See Atul Gawande, *The Checklist Manifesto* (New York, NY: Picador), 162.

144 **History** - Kanban was invented in 1952 as a factory process that pulled work in progress as a team could handle it. See Masaaki Imai, *Kaizen (ky'zen): The Key to Japan's Competitive Success* (New York City, NY: McGraw-Hill, 1991), 89.

145 Confusing capability and capacity would be equally egregious as assuming work and movement are synonymous. Yet, the two have a striking resemblance. A general warning has been expressed by multiple Lean founders who distinguish between work and movement. Ishikawa explains how the word "work" shares the same Chinese word as "movement."

146 Jim Benson & Tonianne Demaria Barry, *Personal Kanban; Mapping Work, Navigating Life* (Seattle, WA: Modus Cooperandi Press, 2011), 49.

147 Ibid., 51.

148 J. M. Juran, *Juran on Leadership for Quality: An Executive Handbook* (Florence, MA: Free Press, 1989), 79.

149 See Stanford model of Professional Fulfillment: https://wellmd.stanford.edu/about/model-external.html

150 Collin McLoughlin & Toshihiko Miura, *True Kaizen: Management's Role in Improving Work Climate and Culture* (Boca Raton, FL: CRC, 2018), 6.

151 Ibid., 23.

152 Daniel Markovitz, *A Factory of One: Applying Lean Principles to Banish Waste and Improve your Personal Performance* (Boca Raton: CRC Press, 2012), 80.

153 Shingeo Shingo, *A Study of the Toyota Production System* (Boca Raton, FL: Routledge, 1989), 186.

154 Daniel Markovitz, *A Factory of One: Applying Lean Principles to Banish Waste and Improve your Personal Performance* (Boca Raton: CRC Press, 2012), 34.

155 Shingeo Shingo, *A Study of the Toyota Production System* (Boca Raton, FL: Routledge, 1989), 24.

156 Jim Benson & Tonianne Demaria Barry, *Personal Kanban; Mapping Work, Navigating Life* (Seattle, WA: Modus Cooperandi Press, 2011), 33.

157 Daniel Markovitz, *A Factory of One: Applying Lean Principles to Banish Waste and Improve your Personal Performance* (Boca Raton: CRC Press, 2012), 110.

158 Let me be clear – I am not encouraging you to assign them to the ticket on your visual task board. This can sow distrust and frustrate non-technical users. The reminder is for you to reach out, not for them. We must be careful to avoid infringing on the personal work management of others without invitation.

159 Jeffrey K. Liker & George Trachilis, *Developing Lean Leaders at All Levels: A Practical Guide* (Jacksonville, FL: Lean Leadership Institute Publications, 2014), 97.

Chapter 7

Technology

The term "technology" refers to any tool, whether physical, mental, rhetorical, or digital, which a person uses to reach a certain goal. It is an integral piece in our journey of empowerment and efforts to transform a culture. In his book *The 4 Stages of Psychological Safety*, Timothy Clark segments the stages of organizational change into three stages: cultural, behavioral, and technical.[1] In our language, it contributes to the success of a *system*, the development of a *person*, and the sustainability of a *process*.

But technology is not the reason a system, person, or process is successful. Each tool is a *vehicle* for the movement of existing energy, not the source of energy. It is the car we drive in, and it relies on the infrastructure of roadways (system), the expertise of the driver (people), and the laws of the road (process). All three of these conditions must first be met before getting behind the wheel or we risk an accident. That is why we purposefully waited until the end of this book to introduce the various tools that leaders can use in their Lean journey. So many organizations have experienced ten-car pileups and traffic accidents because they start by defining Lean by its tools instead of the underlying philosophy that allows each tool to result in success.

We must reframe common Lean tools around the Lean Empowerment System. Some of them will remain unchanged, but others must undergo a transformation toward the new telos, or end, of empowerment. This chapter is organized as both an appendix of tools and a linear flow of ideas. It is split up into two sections: tools for accountability and tools for personal development. Feel free to jump around from tool to tool or read straight through.

DOI: 10.4324/9781032644134-10

Tools for Accountability

Frontline Staff: Data

Data and standards are the two prerequisites for measuring improvement. Data objectively measures stability and progress. Standard work subjectively documents the current best way to achieve stability as measured by the data. We must use a combination of both to measure our progress or we cannot prove an improvement happened. Let us follow the progression from a system without data, to the role of data in the Lean Production System, and finally to the Lean Empowerment System.

Like the absence of standards, **a system without data** must rely on a single leader's gut feelings or instinct to spark the need for change. Strategy goes where the wind blows, and everyone falls in line. An organization that throws the dice of chance can catch a lucky break, later receiving the title of "innovative" or "disruptive." But, like heroism, the leader of change in this setting will seek out the next big idea in the depths of her gut, hoping to hit another vein of inspiration. The deeper she digs, the more obscure the ideas are. And, eventually, gut instinct will fail the seeker and those around her. The unpredictability of working with such a leader can take its toll. Calculated leaders, adverse to the risk of chance, are cast out from her inner circle of influence. The inspirational leader surrounds herself with others who affirm her ideas, often to a fault, or without challenge. The entire organizational culture can quickly divulge to a place where statistical control is a myth and measurable improvement is impossible.

In response to this extreme, but familiar, example, organizations will seek out a *Production System* to inject consistency under the mantle of data. These Lean or Six Sigma programs preach data literacy as the first lesson of education. They follow a simple mantra: "Many of our problems will subside if staff only understand the data." And although frontline staff are included in the many Lean or Six Sigma sessions, like process mapping or rapid improvement events, they do not co-own the data with leadership. It remains a tool of control.

In these settings, we see organizations adding a controller between those making the decision and those feeling the heat of the decision.[2] A study in the Netherlands tracked energy usage between houses to determine the most effective tool or method for lowering energy usage. The researchers studied the effects of education and incentives on energy level but saw little justifiable impact. Then they experimented with the placement of a thermostat within a home. Consider a house with central air and heat: the furnace is located out of sight in a basement or ground floor, and a thermostat is mounted in a public space, such as a living room or dining room. Now compare two styles of design, one where sensors are placed on the *main level* and others where they are placed in the *basement*. The researchers found that families living in the house with a thermostat in the living room had *one-third* lower usage levels than the houses with a thermostat in the basement.[3] The placement of the thermostat had greater impact over energy consumption than any education or program.

Unfortunately, in many traditional Production Systems, staff are placed in houses where the thermostat, or access to data, is on a different level of the house. Only management has access, and staff must wait for leaders to communicate it, which is rarely scheduled on a regular cadence. Also, leaders tend to bring problems to staff after they have already erupted in a ball of fire, expecting quick extinguishment. The system is not made to communicate directly with those feeling the heat as it rises, and the results suffer. Energy consumption increases, and results decrease.

An Empowerment System removes the controller and creates a direct link between the furnace and thermostat. It welcomes frontline staff into the same room as the sensor to watch the fluctuations in live time and self-adjust as needed. All in the name of self-control. This shows, according to Juran, that "before embarking on any plan of motivating the work force to do good work, upper management should determine *the extent to which the workers are in a state of self-control.*"[4] He continues: "the concept of self-control is also universal. It applies to everyone in the company, from the CEO to the worker level, inclusive. The importance of the self-control concept goes beyond its value in establishing clear responsibility and ownership: self-control is a necessary prerequisite to motivation."[5]

One popular example of a sensor is a Daily Management Board. Daily Management Boards are a classic example of a pull system: staff need not wait until a weekly or monthly meeting to have data pushed down from leadership. It is always available. This form of daily management lets them see it and own it.[6] But the board is only effective as part of a larger system. It poses an opportunity for staff to observe local variation (the 20%) but assumes the presence of Standard Work (the 80%). Staff must have an opportunity to challenge both. Without Standard Work, the board risks being perceived as a tool of control under the disguise of self-control. It is another way for managers to achieve their desired results. Only when supported by a comprehensive Kaizen suggestion system can it contribute to true empowerment.

Although the exact format of the board will differ by organization or consultant, a truly impactful board must answer three questions:

1. How are we doing?	Data
2. Who is doing what?	Job Duty Assignment
3. How do we get better?	Improvement Methodology (PDCA, Kata, etc.)

In answering these questions, the board goes beyond simple daily management. It is ultimately a source of learning, a classroom. Data tells a story. And we must learn how to listen. Some scholars even argue how the board should be titled a "Daily Learning Board" because staff must learn how to read it over time and translate it into their own language.

Let us now explore three parts of the board to better understand accountability on the frontline.

Data

Like a story, data is more effective when it is *physical*. Consider theater or spoken word poetry: language takes a new and more robust form. Or contemplate the Incarnation of Jesus: The Gospel writer John explains, "The Word became flesh and dwelt among us" (John 1:14). God's ability to connect with His creation was dramatically improved when He became incarnate in our form. Like these examples we must each bring the story of data alive. Japanese train conductors follow a process called "point and call" where they point and call out steps in a process to increase their likelihood of doing it right.[7] Think about the last time you typed in a credit card number for an online purchase. You probably spoke it out loud to confirm to yourself that it was correct before pushing "Buy." In a similar way, staff find value in seeing and calling out data to make it tangible. Our minds can better grasp the story of data when we can touch it or see it. That is a primary reason why the board must remain physical instead of digital.

A Daily Management Board also connects metrics with process knowledge at the front lines.[8] Imagine a team who realizes their process time is 20-30 seconds below average, and their error rates are above average. The resulting action is simple: use the wiggle room to increase process time by an average of 10 seconds to decrease the error rate. But without the proper guidance, data can send the wrong messages like "work harder" or "work faster," when, in fact, it can say quite the opposite. Reaching statistical control may require staff to slow down or work less.

A final benefit of the Daily Management Board is the conversion of lag measures into lead measures. A team should not bother to set up a process of daily management if the metrics are only available on a weekly or monthly basis. The longer the lag between action and measurement, the more space people can fill with their own narrative. We each tend to fabricate a story in the absence of objectivity. This is because, according to Masaaki Imai, process-oriented metrics have rarely been available to Western leaders.[9] We rely on financial month-end data compared to budget instead of asking the hard question, "how do we know in real-time if our decisions are causing the results we desire?" It is the responsibility of leadership to lasso the data and pull it closer to home.

Job Duty Assignment

According to Juran, "delegation is meaningless unless we have first created the conditions prerequisite to 'self-control.'"[10] In other words, accountability requires data. A responsibility matrix, more commonly known as a RACI matrix, is a common tool to understand and assign the roles of staff:

- **R: Responsible**: A sponsor who asked for the process and gets credit when it succeeds or takes the fall when it doesn't.
- **A: Accountable**: One single person who is assigned to *do* the process.
- **C: Consulted**: Stakeholders who are subject matter experts and provide context when asked by those who are Responsible or Accountable.
- **I: Informed**: Stakeholders who are given updates on the process but do not contribute.

Many leaders struggle with the idea that *only one* person can be accountable in a process. Now, this is not to argue that a task must be done by that one person, but that a single person is assigned to bring an update to the following project call. The project manager doesn't care who does the task or how it is done. All she wants to do is check it off on time. Project managers are specifically taught by PMI (Project Management Institute) to assign one person to a task in a project plan. She uses the Work Breakdown Structure (WBS), an itemized list of tasks and people assigned, as the backbone of a project plan. It is used to elicit the work to be done by each team in their own words. Next, the stakeholders are accountable to the project manager, and the project manager is accountable to the sponsor, who is responsible for the project. Although we want the entire team to share accountability for the success or failure of a project, it starts at a micro level. Here, the project plan is key. It helps the entire team visualize the roadmap of tasks that lie ahead.

I commonly see two self-imposed limitations come to light when teams start using a Daily Management Board to visualize job duty assignment. The first is unlevel loads, and the second is what I call the "everyone does everything" model.

First, a team is forced to reevaluate its task list when someone who is usually accountable is out sick, on vacation, or the team starts to use a Daily Management Board. These situations reveal a strange correlation between staff who hoard tasks and staff who are cynical about doing too much work. This self-inflicted perfectionism is rooted in fear and breeds further cynicism among the rest of the team. The perfectionist doesn't feel supported, often citing elements of unfairness, and others feel untrusted. I have seen this in departments that have a seasoned staff member sur-rounded by more recent hires. Their self-worth and seniority are tied up with their tasks and releasing them may be a challenge. Although we must leave space for specialization and expertise, staff must grow accustomed to trading accountability. Keep in mind that one way to engage the perfection-ist or veteran member is to invite them to slowly mentor and train others in the different tasks. This respects and values their experience while sharing the accountability.

More common than the perfectionist is the team of "team players" where "everyone does everything." Now, this isn't bad, per se, but it isn't the best. A common adage goes, "if everyone does everything, nobody does any-thing." This cuts to the core of accountability. Imagine a team of three registration staff who have identified 9 tasks for their role. If "everyone does everything," each person has nine tasks. But pull back the sheets, and you find that one or two people likely own each task and the others help as needed. Someone is probably hiding in the ambiguity, getting away with doing less work, while others take on more work assuming in good faith that they are supported.

These teams appear busy and productive but participate in a form of "task-thrashing." They self-induce chaos and hinder innovative thinking. It is only when our assigned tasks reach completion that we can focus on improvement. And the roots of this problem go deep: it is based on a long-standing belief from hourly production systems that staff are paid for their time, not for their contribution or expertise. "Everyone doing everything" takes longer and keeps the entire team looking busy. It is a form of job security. And it also has roots in our glorification of multi-tasking. Recall our section in Chapter 6 on multi-tasking and switch-tasking. The word itself is a misnomer; humans cannot multi-task. But it makes us feel productive. The fact that both multi-tasking and busyness are positive shows us how far we are from culturally tackling this issue.

Alternatively, if staff rotated job duties, they could each do three tasks for a week, then rotate the next week. They can still help each other in situations when the one task is simply too much, but as an exception, not the rule. The variation can cut through monotony, create a culture of fairness, and give everyone a chance to learn.

Although assigning job duties on a board may seem elementary, it is the easiest way to recognize unlevel loads and help assign accountability. From personal experience, I can vouch how a simple rotating task list in my childhood home kept my three brothers and I from fighting. More importantly, it helped my parents remove themselves from the situation and set clear expectations. It is a step in the direction away from management dependence and toward empowering frontline staff to assign job duties at a peer level.

Improvement Methodology

Let us oversimplify the story of data into three principles:

1. Know the objectives.
2. Know whether the objectives are met.
3. Change performance if the objectives are not met.

We now move to the third and final part of the learning board: improvement, or changing performance if objectives are not met. The entire board up to this point has been managed by the frontline, but improvement is the responsibility of both staff and management. According to Deming, "If you hold someone to a goal, you must provide the resources to attain it."[11] Staff can only do their job. Leadership is responsible for quality.[12] In the presence of data, and the absence of a cogent improvement methodology, staff tend to participate in "rule beating:" do anything to hit a score or measure. This does not encourage a system view or address cross-functional issues.[13] They may create workarounds, which tend to cause other problems, and prevent process improvement.[14] Or they cheat the system for the sake of looking good.

Modern Lean methods like Kata, PDCA, and A3s are more useful at the local level than the system level. Backed by a Suggestion System, Peer Experts, and Standard Work, each local team can start to identify nuances in the data and impact the processes within their sphere of influence. The goal is learning, not improvement. But staff will inevitably learn their way to better results. Although it may take months for staff to arrive at the same conclusion managers have been sharing in staff meetings, they now own it and call it their own. Sustainable change requires ownership.

Leadership: Strategic Framework

Strategy is standard work for executive leadership. It is more than the musings of a leader or the published Mission Statement of an organization. Like Standard Work, it must be documented, circulated, and reviewed annually. Lean Production Systems call this Hoshin Kanri, literally translated as "compass management."[15] It follows a top-down process of setting annual goals with the rollup of local goals that are reviewed monthly. The strategy is a benchmark for success, a guide for prioritization of work, and helps leaders delegate to their teams.

Patrick Lencioni, popular author, speaker, and founder of The Table Group, encourages every leadership team to create a Strategic Framework that outlines a team's commitment to its goals. Lencioni's framework is like Hoshin Kanri with a human touch. It flows from intangible ideas to tangible goals, as outlined by six questions:

- Why do we exist?
- How do we behave?
- What do we do?
- How will we succeed?
- What is most important, right now?
- Who must do what?[16]

The development of strategy is the most spiritual experience a secular corporation can have. For this reason, we must orchestrate its development and invite leaders to enter a space of vulnerability. The facilitator cannot simply inspire with excitement and energy; they must be attentive to the human spirit and the source of creativity within each person. Only then can an executive team co-create an artistic expression worthy of contemplation. A strategic retreat is a welcome reset for leaders to connect on a personal level and collaborate toward something bigger than themselves. Everyone is willing to work toward the greater good, but our default mode is to protect our own. Creating a strategic framework forces leaders to talk across the aisle and place the individual goals of their departments in the context of the entire organization.

Strategy is notably different from a run of the mill idea or inspirational quip. It is "holy," or in Hebrew, *kodesh*, which is derived from the word Kadash that means "set apart for a specific purpose." Consider scripture, the tomes of famous authors, or bars of neatly woven poetry: a reader can glean different meanings upon each reading. It will change depending on one's stage in life, a new child, a change in employment, or simply their mood that day. Truly inspired literature will change with the seasons. And it is our job to receive it graciously. In theology this practice is called *Lectio Divina* or "divine reading," which is broken down into four steps:

1. Read (*Lectio*): Read the text. Allow a certain word or phrase to jump out to you.
2. Meditate (*Meditatio*): Reread the same passage. Focus again on the same word or phrase.
3. Pray (*Oratio*): Use the word or phrase to start a conversation with God.
4. Contemplate (*Contemplatio*): Simply dwell in the presence of God. Oscillate between meditation (listening) and prayer (talking) to connect the word or phrase to a purpose (telos). Ask, "Why does this stand out to me? How am I being called?"

Each layer of the organization has a discernible role in the Lean Empowerment System. Leaders use a Strategic Framework to inspire direction. Peer Experts collaborate with the Process Improvement Team to create and improve Standard Work as they hear the voice of staff. And Frontline Staff huddle daily around a Learning Board to read the story of data, assign job duties, and learn their way to improvement. We must apply the tools at our disposal to the growth and development of the organization and its people. Let us now turn to focus on the tools of personal development.

Tools for Personal Development

Personal: Work–Life Integration

The subject of work–life balance is experiencing a renaissance in the workplace due to the growing number of Millennial and Gen Z leaders. The loudest voices in this camp demand a type of work–life balance that more closely resembles "work–life separation:" Staff expect to go off the grid and shut off work once they clock out. But our current technological climate has made this dream unrealistic. We carry our email in our pocket. More and more cell numbers replace work numbers in email signatures or business cards. And our personal devices are required for multi-factor authentication. Is this flavor of work–life balance realistic when we are so attached to our screens?

Let us start to answer this question by better understanding the idea of "balance" within the term "work–life balance." Imagine a tight-rope walker or slackliner: does she ever reach a state of balance as she moves from one pole to the next? I would argue not. As an experienced slackliner, I teach newcomers that true balance is a myth. We are in a perpetual state of falling, followed by counterbalance after counterbalance. We compensate for even the slightest change with another change until each reaction becomes a calculated preparation for the next reaction. Balance exists only as a channeling of energy from one state of falling into the next, catching ourselves long enough to take the next step, or sometimes landing on the ground, only to get back up again.

Now, with the image of a slackliner in mind, let us reconsider the idea of work–life balance. A new model must allow us to maintain a healthy compartmentalization of work without completely severing from it. The two worlds of work and home are not two worlds, but one. We know there are benefits to bringing the energy we receive from work home with us, channeling our productivity and positivity into our families. The downside comes when negative energy in the form of anxiety, frustration, or excess work is also brought home. Doctors call this "pajama time." The same energy goes in the other direction, from home to work. We bring a human face from our roles as parents, spouses, or siblings to our work. The energy from our hobbies can funnel into our projects. But we also risk bringing supercharged emotions from family or spousal interactions into the objectivity of the workplace.

This two-laned transference of energy is defined as "work–life integration." It is tailored to knowledge workers in a technological world and replaces the outdated and unrealistic idea of "work–life balance." With the right system in place, surrounded by the right people, and equipped with the right tools, we can allow the best of ourselves to bleed over. We are best when we allow ourselves to be whole.

Relational: Mentorship

Mentorship is continual improvement (kaizen) of the self. A mentor helps a mentee connect the musings of her head (intellect), the labor of her hands (work), and the longings of her heart (purpose). She is a catalyst of preexisting gifts and a coach of new skills. Although the goals of mentorship vary from relationship to relationship, one of three outcomes is common:

- Activate leadership qualities within people who are not active leaders.
- Dispel imposter syndrome in leaders who don't feel like it.
- Humble leaders that have an inflated view of themselves.

Each conversation is an act of "equipping" leaders with the tools they need.[17] And each mentoring relationship is a bond that strengthens the DNA of the empowerment system. This makes mentorship more than simply a conversation between two people. It is based on tested methods and research. Ken Blanchard & Claire Diaz-Ortiz explain in *One Minute Mentoring* how a mentoring relationship flows from essence to form. In their words, "essence is all about sharing heart-to-heart and finding common values. Form is about structure."[18] A meaningful relationship must start with essence and eventually move to form. Then it can oscillate comfortably between the two.

The *essence* of mentorship is basic human connection. And it is a process of discovery. We reveal essence when we ask simple questions like: What is your role? What are your interests? What brings you joy? The goal is to find base commonalities as human beings before exploring the heavier topics of meaning and purpose. Our dreams set the direction of our conversation.

The *form* of mentorship includes clear expectations and guardrails for both the mentor and mentee. It also gives the mentor a fallback of questions and tools. The stage of form is riddled with moments of helping the mentees voice their ideas, maybe for the first time, and handing the mentor important information to explore. It is about reframing the mentees' experiences and creating connections.

Each system must organize its mentorship program around its culture. But there are a few tips that can help first-time mentors. For example, it is better to offer mentorship to a small group of leaders, preferably Peer Experts, who are primed for rich dialogue. Opening the floodgates to all frontline staff can overwhelm the newly christened mentors and saturate the capability of the system. But over time, as the base of available mentors grows, and the system grows more comfortable with the idea of mentorship, it can expand to a wider base. A system will become more efficient as it multiplies its leaders, level loading the difficult work of emotional resilience and spiritual growth. The opposite of multiplication is division, or the belief that one leader can do everything. And failure to invest in the growth of leaders is the ultimate waste, a waste of potential. It is our responsibility to establish sustainable systems that multiply more than divide.

Communal: Digital Collaboration Platforms

The explosion of social media platforms over the past few decades is indicative of a growing interest in digital connection. We no longer rely on water cooler conversations, after work gatherings, or phone calls for our work relationships. Rather, we depend on the capabilities of digital platforms for asynchronous communication. Almost every organization uses a digital collaboration platform that allows members to post publicly in groups, video chat one-on-one, set up team meetings, and collaborate asynchronously on cloud-based documents, to name a few capabilities. The opportunities for collaboration are seemingly endless for those who know how to engage.

Each organization must reflect on the most effective way to structure the digital platforms to maximize interactions between peers, increase usage of reference documents, and improve compliance with standards. The opportunities of technology are as limited as one's imagination. Setting up a group for each role in an organization is a natural and easy way to spark dialogue. It is like putting everyone in the same room; conversation will naturally arise.

Notes

1 Timothy R. Clark, *The 4 Stages of Psychological Safety: Defining the Path to Inclusion and Innovation* (Oakland, CA: Berrett-Koehler Publishers, Inc., 2020), 97–98.

2 Frances Westley, Brenda Zimmerman, and Michael Patton, *Getting to Maybe: How the World is Changed* (Toronto, ON: Vintage Canada, 2007), 132.

3 Donella H. Meadows, *Thinking in Systems* (Chelsea, VT: Chelsea Green Publishing, 2008), 109.

4 J. M. Juran, *Juran on Leadership for Quality: An Executive Handbook* (Florence, MA: Free Press, 1989), 276.

5 Ibid., 148.

6 Daniel Markovitz, *A Factory of One: Applying Lean Principles to Banish Waste and Improve your Personal Performance* (Boca Raton: CRC Press, 2012), 93.

7 James Clear, *Atomic Habits: An Easy & Proven Way to Build Good Habits & Break Bad Ones* (New York, NY: Avery Publishing, 2018), 63.

8 Peter Senge, *The Fifth Discipline* (Manhattan, NY: Random House Business, 2006), 364.

9 Masaaki Imai, *Kaizen (ky'zen): The Key to Japan's Competitive Success* (New York City, NY: McGraw-Hill, 1991), 39.

10 J. M. Juran, *Managerial Breakthrough* (New York, NY: McGraw-Hill Book Co., 1995), 206.

11 W. Edwards Deming, *The New Economics: For Industry, Government, Education* (Cambridge, MA: The MIT Press, 2018), 41.

12 Ibid., 16.

13 Donella H. Meadows, *Thinking in Systems* (Chelsea, VT: Chelsea Green Publishing, 2008), 137.

14 Amy C. Edmondson, *The Fearless Organization: Creating Psychological Safety in the Workplace for Learning, Innovation, and Growth* (Hoboken, NJ: John Wiley & Sons, 2019), 37.

15 https://www.infoq.com/news/2017/03/hoshin-kanri-toyota/

16 I highly recommend the following book: Patrick Lencioni, *The Advantage: Why Organizational Health Trumps Everything Else in Business* (San Francisco, CA: Jossey-Bass, 2012).

17 John C. Maxwell, *Mentoring 101: What Every Leader Needs to Know* (Nashville, TN: HarperCollins Leadership, 2008), 58.

18 Ken Blanchard and Claire Diaz-Ortiz, *One Minute Mentoring: How to Find and Work with a Mentor—And Why You'll Benefit from Being One* (New York, NY: William Morrow, 2017), 30.

Conclusion

There is a French riddle that illustrates the compounding rate at which culture changes.

> Imagine a pond with a single lily pad.
> Each day, the lily pad doubles.
> The entire pond is covered in lily pads on day thirty.
> On what day is the pond half covered?
>
> Day twenty-nine.
> Not day fifteen, as many guess.

Recall our thesis from the Introduction: **Lean must evolve from a Production System to an Empowerment System**. This evolution will not happen overnight. It will take time to balance the scales of **Respect for People** and **Continuous Improvement**. But thankfully, the elements already exist. Just as the pond starts with a lily pad, we start with a rich history of primary and secondary sources that have paved the way for a Lean Empowerment System. The chapters in this book have unearthed the whisperings of Empowerment throughout the vast body of Lean knowledge. It was always there, but the existing system was not ready to receive it. And over time, as more secondary sources were published, we became buried under the same ideas, repeated, and repackaged, further away from the original desires of the first engineers who spread Lean before it was called "Lean." We succumbed to the **Vices of Production**, growing in our dependence on **heroes, management, projects, and urgency**, unaware of the long-term effects. But now the tide has turned. The workforce has changed. And a Lean Production System can no longer serve our modern employees. It is time to evolve. Equipped with the **Virtues of**

DOI: 10.4324/9781032644134-11

Empowerment – ordinariness, peer problem solving, Kaizen, and design – we can propose something new into the history of Lean.

The Lean Empowerment System is a salve for the wounds caused by Lean Production Systems. It is **a self-organizing body of Lateral Leaders who improve Standard Work in a Kaizen Suggestion System**. And we experience it as embodied and incarnate within our **systems**, **people**, **processes**, and **technologies**. Leaders must take the time to discern each layer of simplicity. Only then can complexity make sense.

We have encountered many new forms of waste along the journey of Empowerment that are mere footnotes in a Production System. What we now know to be the greatest form of waste among knowledge workers also happens to be a late addition to the original eight wastes as defined by Lean scholars: **the waste of human potential**. According to Alfie Kohn, "we have a moral obligation to make work meaningful and remove meaningless waste."[1] Staff are good at identifying other forms of waste in a process, but they require support to recognize their own potential. To do this, the role of a leader must change in the face of empowerment. She must focus not on the **destination** or the **journey**, but the **journeyers** beside her.

Let me end with a reflection: our entire career oscillates between action, the *work* of work, and collaboration, the *being* of work. We hear this beautifully proclaimed in the Gospel of Luke 10:38-42:

> Now as they went on their way, he entered a certain village, where a woman named Martha welcomed him into her home. She had a sister named Mary, who sat at the Lord's feet and listened to what he was saying. But Martha was distracted by her many tasks; so she came to him and asked, "Lord, do you not care that my sister has left me to do all the work by myself? Tell her then to help me." But the Lord answered her, "Martha, Martha, you are worried and distracted by many things; there is need of only one thing. Mary has chosen the better part, which will not be taken away from her."

Martha represents action. Mary represents collaboration. Although we are quick to praise Mary, Jesus would have never entered the house if Martha had not called out to him. He would not have eaten if Martha had not prepared a meal. The conditions for Mary's ability to sit and listen to Jesus would not exist without the work of Martha. Although it is the better part, it is not the only part, and rarely the first part.

Be Martha. Then Mary. Evolve from Production to Empowerment. And love those on the journey.

Note

1 Alfie Kohn, *Punished by Rewards: The Trouble with Gold Stars, Incentive Plans, A's, Praise, and Other Bribes* (Boston, MA: Mariner Books, 1993), 189.

Index

Pages in *italics* refer to figures, and pages followed by "n" refer to notes.

Printed in the United States
by Baker & Taylor Publisher Services